Praise for
Go with the Fat Cats

"I love your episodic way of telling your story, each episode with an insight into your character and the way of the Orthodox Greeks. 'When we see charity as a privilege, rather than a duty, we gain much more from our good works than we lose in performing them.' Beautiful."
—**David V. Hicks**, author of *Norms and Nobility*

"My early years in Chicago in an Irish American family are so much like the beautifully written stories in this unique, highly readable book that brings together a psychological, and personal narrative about the influence of Greek culture and family. George Zimmar's writing challenges readers to reflect on the values and perspectives of their own life experience and. culture. Highly recommended."
—**Barry McCarthy, Ph.D.** author of *Enhancing Couple Sexuality*

"In the 1950s' Chicago, the teenage son of Greek immigrants struggles to deal with the ambivalence and challenges of his ethnic identity. Is he Greek or American? He wants to honor his glorious Greek heritage and strict Greek father, but the pull of sexy American girls and the American way of life are too strong to ignore. How will he find his identity, love, and acceptance of who he is?"
—**Ben Kyriagis**, author of *Don't Marry an American*

COMMENTS FROM READERS

*Nicely done—besides the writing, the depth of tracing
and developing family history.*

*Laconia, Beautiful story. Aikateri-
ni Marouda was either 1st or 2nd cousins with my
great great grandmother Aikaterini Marouda!!!*

*Wonderful story. Oddly enough, my father's roots in Ri-
chea near Molaoi can be traced back it is said to a Kokoris
(Kokkoos maybe) who killed an Ottoman tax collector.*

Keep your roots alive congratulations.

Lakonia !!!! My dad . . . Tsouni, Sparti.

A marvelous storyteller.

Hamartia was very interesting.

*Gives me a real sense of what you lived through
as a child and teenager. So sad and so honest.*

*I continue to enjoy your essays and articles—Hamartia is particularly
thought provoking. Irony and paradox. I loved reading this story.*

*Hamartia is the most powerful and meaningful
article I've read. Thank you for sharing. Very well written.*

The Hamartia article was great! I really enjoyed it.

Dr. George Zimmar is adjunct Senior Professor of Psychology at Pace University and has published many articles in peer referenced journals and Greek Ancestry blog. Formerly, he was Director and Publisher at publishing companies that included Rowman and Littlefield and Routledge Press. He holds a doctorate from the University at Buffalo, post-doctoral fellowship at MIT, and chaired the Psychology Departments at Grinnell and Briarcliff Colleges. Zimmar is an Archon of the Order of St. Andrew the Apostle and served on the Parish Council of the Church of Our Saviour, Rye, NY, for 50 years. Zimmar and his wife, the elegant and gracious Doulie Pappas Zimmar, are the parents of two adult children and grandparents of five.

GO WITH THE FAT CATS

YES BOOKS
Briarcliff, New York

Hardback ISBN: 979-8-9883857-0-7
Paperback ISBN: 979-8-9883857-1-4

Book cover and interior design by Jess LaGreca, Mayfly Design

Library of Congress Catalog Number: 2023909321

First Printing: 2023

Printed in the United States of America

GO WITH THE FAT CATS

A GREEK AMERICAN YOUTH
IN PURSUIT OF IDENTITY AND LOVE

GEORGE P. ZIMMAR

For my mother, Sophia, who gave me life, and
for my wife, Doulie, who saved my life.

FAMILY TREE

George Peter Zimmar

Anagnostis Zymaras (1801–?)   Panagiotis Kanellis (1802–c1848)
(Great great grandmother?)   Sousana (?–1895)

|

Athanasios Zoumaras (1828–?) Athanasios Kanellis (1836–1905)
Panagiota Rorri   Aikaterini Maroudas (1844–1910)

|

Gioryios Zoumaras (1855–1944) Adamantios Kanellis (1870–1951)
Panagiota Karkas (1862–1936)   Garyfalia Doulfas (1884–1966)

|

Panagiotis Zymaras (1888–1986) Sophia Kanellis (1914–2006)
[Peter Zimmar]

|

M. March 13, 1937

|

George Peter Zimmar (1937)   Arhondoula Pappas (1945)

|

M. November 20, 1971

David Zimmar (1940–1978)
(Brother)
Peggy Zimmar (1943) (Sister)

INTRODUCTION

During the time, I set pen to paper to write this story of growing up Greek American in Chicago, I began reading Thomas Wolfe's dazzling memoir, *Look Homeward Angel,* recounting his youth in Asheville, North Carolina. The similarities of content in both his and the stories presented here were apparent: tumultuous family search for a better life, unrequited teen love, a death, quest for a richer intellectual life, an aging *paterfamilias* who exercised authority over the family. Nonetheless the contrast could not have been greater, because the homeward souls in my family were Greek immigrants and Wolfe's were native Americans.

"Go with the fat cats!" were the words of my college mentor as I joined a prestigious medical research center to wrest my way into life as a college professor and publisher from my origins as a soda jerk in a Greek American family-owned sweet shop. This volume explores the expression of ethnic identity as the unconscious need to be both part of and apart from the ethnic group into which I was born—a dual mentality that succors and conflicts the *persona.*

Compared to the impoverished of the world, even the poorest of Americans are fat cats. However, for a struggling Greek American immigrant family, the fat cats were those with more education, more security, more well-being, more assets, more integration into the American way of life. Succeeding in whatever they did was a reality that immigrants endeavored to achieve if not for themselves, for their children. The contrast of the social and cultural milieus between the 1950s and 1960s revealed the fault lines of American society. The 1960s marked a turning away from the relative stability of cultural values and religious beliefs of the 1950s to the turmoil of social change, distractions to personal achievement, and decline of religion that followed.

From 47th Street Memories, Tales of the Park Manor Sweet Shop, to Travels with My Sister and Wild Berries at Delphi, fat cats large and small are encountered along the way in this memoir that probes the essence of ethnic identity. The qualities that make Greekness unique, such as *philoxenia*, meaning love of the foreign, are about much more than a warm welcome to strangers; it is a complex moral code with deep roots. My loving ambivalence of my Greekness is the thread that runs through this memoir.

However, there is a deeper side to this story, which is not a rejection of my ethnic roots but a keeping of my ethnicity firmly at arm's length. Immigrants' children—whether Jewish, Latino, or Greek—go through this duality of mind with varying degrees of torment. The conflict is one between celebrating one's culture and putting off or dissuading ethnic contact, which is harbored at the unconscious level but expressed consciously. We may marry someone outside of the group and then encourage our spouse to adopt our culture, our values, religion, and cuisine. Ethnic identity that both empowers and constrains personal development is the strand running through this memoir and essays. Double mindedness impedes personal integrity, shrouds the person in conflict, and sometimes has tragic consequences.

Over the years I have accepted invitations to submit articles to the *Journal of Humanistic Psychiatry*. Each issue of the journal covered a specific topic of human interest, including essays on identity, justice, envy, human motives, dreams, transcendence, and truth. These articles, which have been revised for this volume, have brought

me to the conclusion that our ethnicity, our parenting, our upbringing, our childhoods leave indelible marks on our psyches, however
far we strive to stray from where we started. To quote T.S. Eliot, "In
my end is my beginning."

CONTENTS

ESSAYS

Wisdom

Psychology

Reviews

ONE

47TH STREET
MEMORIES

Memory is the diary that we all carry about with us.
—Oscar Wilde

My very earliest recollection was seeing my dad behind bars in a lock-up. Our apartment on New England Avenue was in a well-appointed brick building (after the Great Fire all housing in Chicago was brick) with about 12 apartments on a tree-lined street. The neighbors in the apartment below were elderly and tiresome and often complained that the Greek foreigner's kids—I and my younger brother, David—disturbed their tranquility. Moreover, I am told that as my parents walked from one room to another, the neighbors would strike their ceiling with a broom in protest over the footsteps. We walked shoeless in the apartment, but the complaints continued until the neighbors filed a disorderly conduct complaint with the local judiciary for eviction. Dad came home late one evening to find a police car at the apartment door to take him to jail. Next morning my mom took my brother and me to the police station, where I saw my dad behind bars waiting to go to court.

The judge took one look at the situation—my immigrant parents with small children in a crammed apartment and the elderly, irritable complainants—then angrily dismissed the case and chastised the police for the arrest. Soon after, as I was going down the back steps to play in the yard, the lady neighbor flung open her door and, perhaps to make amends, held up a cookie as a peace offering, which I took. She said, "What do you say?" My response: "Can I have another one?' The door slammed.

PETER AND SOFIA, IN VRONDAMA
WITH IBRAHIM

There is not much of a family record at the time of my birth, nine months after my parents married. After he arranged the marriage of his sister, Stella (1905–1989), to Louis Cotsonis (1891–1960 ca), my father returned to Greece in 1936, leaving his candy story in their charge. My dad, Peter, had spent his life setting up his brother up in business, caring for sister, and supporting his parents, so it was time for him to make a life with a wife and family.

He met my mother, Sophia Kanellis, (1914–2006) at the monastery of Elona, near Kosmas in Peloponnesus. The meeting was arranged by her brother-in-law and my dad's friend, Demetri (Mitso) Kontoyianis, who had a dry sense of humor. When Mitso's handsome and engaging brother-in-law, Christos Kanellis told the family that he was engaged to marry an educated Athenian woman, who could speak four languages (tongues in Greek). Mitso's chauvinist, mocking comment to Christos, "Son, the gods cursed men by giving woman one tongue, you found a woman with four!"

My mom had undertaken a pilgrimage, walking barefoot from Kosmas, past my paternal grandfather's house, on the road to the monastery, to thank the Theotokos for the safe return of her brother, Ioannis from military service in northern Greece. Dad and Sophia spent chaperoned time together at the monastery. Dad asked if he could visit with her in Geraki, her hometown, about 15 kilometers distant and she consented. Dad arrived at Diamandis Kanellis' s home, bearing gifts for the family members. He was quizzed about his family—my paternal grandfather, Gioryios was known in Geraki in that he owned property and a house in a nearby town. My maternal grandmother, Panayiota, had passed away. Sophia and Peter visited his father in the family's second home in the nearby town of Vrondama and Gioryios was approving of her. Dad asked Diamandis for Sophia's hand in marriage and the union was approved. In Greek tradition, the dowry (προίκα) was a necessary prelude to engagement and marriage.

The dowry, an aspect of Greek wedding tradition, is the property that the bride brings into the marriage. Typical of patrilineal

Sophia at Rabat Morocco

societies, the dowry accords value to both the groom and the bride. A well-to-do bride may bring substantial wealth to the marriage, and a poor groom may command a lower dowry in the marriage arrangement. Money or real estate are common forms of dowry. In the film, My Big Fat Greek Wedding, Toula was given a house, next to her family's home, as the dowery. The προίκα is a form of protection for the bride in that she retains possession of the property, and the dowry goes with her in the event of a divorce. While dowries can be traced back to antiquity in Sparta, the practice is in decline among Greeks in today's marriages. However, let's look at what a woman brings to a marriage, beyond the transfer of wealth, as was in my mother's case.

My father sought a soulmate after a lifetime of living alone. Sophia was more than a companion for life; she was his helpmate and brought many gifts to the marriage, primarily, her virtue. She was family oriented, which means that the material, moral, and spiritual needs of their children would be met, as well as Peter's needs. She respected her husband and his family. She would pull her weight in the family business. She was deeply religious and gave to the poor. Sophia gave deeper meaning and purpose to Peter's life and in a sense, she saved his life. "Who can find a virtuous woman? For her price is far above rubies. She would do him good, and not evil, all the days of her life" (Proverbs, 31:10) A virtuous woman is a crown to her husband" (Proverbs, 12:3). Thanks to Sophia, Peter prospered in more ways than one.

Demetri Kontoyianis discussed the dowery with Peter and Sophia's family. Hard currency or gold was not available at the time, so a parcel of land that contained olive trees was the dowry. It was agreed that Sophia's brother Mihael would care for the property. They married in March 1937; Peter was 49, Sophia was 22, and they were a handsome couple. They honeymooned in Athens and Morocco and returned to the United States.

The honeymooners returned to Chicago to find that dad's business was at the point of bankruptcy. Perhaps it was improvident for

Peter to have left his business with his sister and Louis, who had a gambling problem. As a result, Peter went to work for his younger brother, Tom, and we moved into an apartment near his store.

A visit to my Uncle Tom's store involved a series of transit switches from the southeast side of Chicago to the city's northwest. We would walk from Drexel Boulevard's all-white middle-class apartments, board a westbound streetcar at 47th and Cottage Grove Avenue—the border between black and white residences and the route of the annual (since 1929) Bud Billiken Parade, the country's largest African American parade—and ride through the black business section. Army and Lou's Rib Emporium, Casper's Fresh Greens market, Sid Hersh's Cleaners, Horowitz Meats, and a myriad of other stores

PETER NEXT TO MONTCLAIR THEATER

dotted 47th Street on the way to the El that sliced through the city. From there, the elevated cut through Chicago's southside slums, factories, warehouses, and vacant lots and traveled roughly 55 city blocks north to the Grand Avenue exit, which was not far from the stately Water Works Tower built after Chicago was devastated by fire in 1871. A Chicago Surface Line streetcar then carried us west through largely residential areas to the Montclair movie theater, dad and his brother worked in the ice cream parlor next to the theater. The border of Chicago and its Elmwood Park suburb were nearby to the west.

We were a family of four and my brother, David, and I rarely separated, ever embracing each other, and playing together. Perhaps I was holding him to me rather than the other way around. When my mother was pregnant with my sister, Peggy, the discussion on childbirth was muted. Parents at that time did not discuss family matters, especially if these were remotely related to sexuality. Today parents discuss the impending birth with their children to prepare them for the new family member.

As my mom's due date for the birth of our sister neared, arrangements were made to have David stay with my mom's sister Angelike in Valparaiso Indiana, and for me to stay with her cousin Uncle Tom Metos in Chicago. Nothing was said to David or me about these temporary living arrangements, but one day, Dad, David, and I boarded the South Shore train and headed to Indiana, passing through the sooty Gary steel mills and the pastoral farmland beyond to my aunt and uncle's roadside café, gas station, and farm at the intersection of US Routes 6 and Hwy 49.

After lunch at my uncle's cafe, my brother and I went next door to the Standard Oil gas station, fascinated with the working garage and the scores of dead flies frozen to the sticky fly paper strips hanging in the window, when dad came in and said, "We are going home. We have a ride to Chicago with the coffee vendor." I was loaded into the back of the panel truck bearing the aroma of coffee bags, and the truck left—without my brother. Looking out the rear window,

GEORGE AND DAVID, CHICAGO, C. 1941

I saw David with our aunt receding by the roadside. I cried out that I wanted my brother back and broke into tears. Through the waves of my bawling, my dad tried to tell me that the separation was temporary, only until the birth of the baby, but to no avail. I sobbed the 35 miles to Chicago. Later, on July 4, 1978, David was killed in a car accident not far from the road on which we traveled home to Chicago that day. I made the arrangements for the funeral and the mourning afterward without tears. Perhaps it was prescient that I had cried my heart out at losing him as the panel truck carried me and my dad away.

In 1943, we moved from the northwest to the south side of the city to 47th and Drexel Avenue. The Kostakis family, my mother's cousins from Geraki, Greece, the former occupants, transferred the lease to my parents and moved to 76th and Coles in the elegant South Shore neighborhood. The apartment came with a tenant, Mike, who lived in the front bedroom and worked in Mr. Kostakis's liquor store on the south side of town. Post-war housing was tight, so Mike was allowed to remain in his lodgings. The railroad apartment came with a parlor, kitchen, dining room, three bedrooms, and a bathroom with a tub—all lined up along a hallway that traversed the apartment. Michael Papadimitris, a bachelor of about 50 years old, was pear-shaped and humpbacked. He would return to the apartment, go to his room at about 2:00 am, deposit his wallet in the dresser drawer, and sleep until about 9:00 am. Around 10 a.m. he would leave his room, wearing pants and an armless t-shirt, a towel around his shoulders. and made his way down the hall to the bathroom, where he shaved and got ready for the day. Michael was partially bald; his features were Mediterranean, with dark eyes and a prominent hooked nose, but he was pallid from having worked indoors most of his life. Once a week he bathed in the tub. Around noon, he would head for work at the liquor store. Each fortnight Mike entered Rocco's barbershop in the building for a haircut, shave, manicure, and shoeshine. Like Willy's barber in *Death of a Salesman*,

Rocco brushed the hair and dandruff off Mike's coat and made sure his tie was properly placed. Mike would leave the shop all spiffy and ready to take on the world. Like many men without mates, he led a lonely existence. I resolved Mike's solitary life was one that I would not lead. On Fridays, Mike left his rent, $7, on the lamp table next to his room. That modest sum, a dollar a day, closed the gap in our family finances during a difficult period of our lives.

Our new residence was in a large corner apartment building that consisted of about 30 three-bedroom apartments. Each apartment had a 10 x 10' back porch and a storage area in the basement where the laundry was done. On warm days, women would hang the wash out to dry on clotheslines strung in the large backyard. As the city became sootier from car exhaust and the steel mills to the south, the clotheslines were abandoned, and the yard given over to the children in the building for play.

My playmates' ethnic backgrounds were broad: Irish, Italian, Jewish, German. Helena Bloch and her family were in Munich during the war, and Eugene Dinkins' grandparents came to the United States just prior to the onset of war. Sy and Alan Hersh's dad owned the cleaners on 47th street. Todaro's teenage son Anthony had a Cushman Motor Scooter on which he gave rides to the kids in the building. The superintendent, who took pride in caring for the building, was German, and my downstairs buddy, Shelly Gitelman, would converse in Yiddish with Horst, who would reply in German. As a six-year-old, my memory of the place just after we had moved in on a brisk January day with snowflakes swirling in circles was wondering what living in our new home would bring.

The back yard of the apartment teemed with children. There was not a single Greek family in the complex or, for that matter, in the school. Often my mother would call us from the back porch for lunch or dinner. One time I was extremely embarrassed and told my mom that the kids laughed at me when she called me to come upstairs and have some lemon soup. "They said that you were boiling lemons in a pot to make soup."

Mom went to the porch and called out, "Seymour, Eugene, Alan, Sheldon, come upstairs right now." The four boys sheepishly appeared at the back door, and she shuttled them into the kitchen and sat them around the table with my brother David and me. From the pot on the stove, she poured out a cup of egg-lemon (avgolemono) soup, for each boy, which they devoured greedily and held up their cups for seconds. My mother said, "Go home now and give thanks to your mothers for whatever she puts on the table.

After two trying years at St. Ambrose Elementary School, the nuns judged that I was an unfit candidate for a Roman Catholic education. Despite my mother's wishes for religious schooling, I was transferred to the public Shakespeare Elementary School at 46th and Greenwood Avenue, roughly four city blocks from our home. Postwar schools were overcrowded. In a class of seven rows of seven children, I was the 50th pupil, seated next to the pencil sharpener at the window. Eventually I was seated in the last row, seventh seat, when a student was moved to another classroom. My best friends in elementary school were Sidney Bogin, Merton Thayer, and Sheldon Gitelman. Occasionally Eugene Dinkens would break into the pack, but he was weirder than the rest of us nerds. Sidney and I would walk home for lunch. One time we were playing grab the other guy's nuts, roughhousing with each other, and lunging. From her perch at the window, Mrs. Bogin saw what we were doing and from that time on, I was *persona non grata* at the Bogin household and our walks home together ended, but we remained friends. Sidney was a punster par excellence. In class he would make up ads for different products like

"Salada" Tea. His pitch was, "I drinks-a-lotta tea." The class would groan in nonappreciation, but Sidney would go on with the next pun. Another classmate was Anthony Ratcliff, an African American kid. Neighborhood segregation was breaking down, and blacks lived in the building. Anthony and I played chess.

"Aha, checkmate! Gotcha again, Anthony," I gloated. Anthony Ratcliffe was visiting our home, and we were nine-year-old gladiators immersed in a *mano a mano* chess tournament. My mother happened by and called me to the other room as Anthony was setting up the chessboard for another game. "Your manner is rude to your guest. You have a duty to be a good host, Gioryo. We are privileged by his visit. Now I want you to go back and allow Anthony to do better in the next game. Cookies and milk in 15 minutes." Through such life lessons, we absorb what *philoxenia*, love (*philo*) of the stranger (*xenos*) means. But what was my mom thinking when she asked me to throw the game?

Philoxenia is a distinctive feature of Greek family life, welcoming a stranger, especially a traveler, away from their home. Philoxenia is about much more than a warm welcome; it is a complex moral code with deep roots. Christ teaches us to love our neighbor as ourselves; this was the basis of my mom's reprimand. However, the Orthodox Church's deepest traditions also instruct us that not only do we have a duty to the poor or the stranger but that it is our privilege to serve them. In my mother's mind, by giving up a game I was giving thanks to Anthony for the honor of his visit to our home and laying the groundwork for our friendship.

How we approach our charitable activities shapes our conduct and defines what we gain from performing these acts. Do we view serving the needs of the poor merely as a duty to be fulfilled? An obligation to be discharged with alacrity by writing a check to have done with it until the next inevitable request for financial support. When as dutiful donors we give within our means to sustain the operations and mission of a school, hospital, church, or old age home, should not this be enough?

Certainly, the smallest generous act is more than enough for a charity—from volunteering time to its program, giving a ride to the disabled, substitute teaching a class, serving one day on a committee. These charitable actions count, and good comes from them. So, does it make a difference if they are performed as a duty or a privilege since the result is the same? Sure, it does. Different motives attend these mindsets. A duty is viewed as an obligation, while a privilege becomes a benefit. With an obligation something is taken from us, be it time or money. However, when we see charity as a privilege, we gain much more from our good works than we lose in performing them. The stranger who visits our home deserves to be celebrated as well. Honestly, I do not recall if Anthony won the next game as my mom requested. Most likely not. But I do remember the warm cookies and milk he and I shared.

"Butch! Come on, boy!" From the middle of the open field, the dog, my dog for that hour, would prick his ears, turn, and come charging at me full of joy and fellowship. Two elderly sisters in our building paid me 25 cents to walk their dog every day, rain, or shine. Butch and I would head out for the wide world of interesting sniffs and places to pee and poop. Butch was a crossbreed between a German Shepherd and Doberman Pinscher, quite a formidable animal. But to Butch, I was the was leader of the pack.

Greeks in Greece do not keep animals as pets in their homes. A dog belongs in the field tending sheep or goats and protecting them from predators, not as a family member. Our family tried small pets, like a canary that died in the first blast of winter, or numerous overfed goldfish that also died before a relationship could be established. We had a kitten, Cutie, my sister's pet, which enjoyed the stimulation of her three rambunctious playmates. Cutie would take off on her nightly search for rodents, but came home one day and died, possibly of rat poison. Dave and I put on our uniforms and toy guns and marched with Peggy to the vacant lot where a mansion once stood; we gave Cutie a military funeral and burial in a pit, which we covered with a flat tile. Cutie had a tomb. Days later Dave and I went back to the hole that we dropped Cutey in and discovered that the effects of death on the body were ghastly.

The daily walk with Butch continued for about a year. Then, without warning, the elderly ladies decided to move. The neighborhood was becoming too threatening for them. There were break-ins of apartments in the building, so their concerns were justified. Even the presence of Butch did not provide the required security. Aside from learning that the love of an animal is a profound experience, I also determined that if you love your job, money for work is secondary compensation.

47th Street was my avenue of dreams. Each day on the way home from school, I would stop at the bookshop window and read the titles of the books on display and wonder about the contents. The Hardy Boys book series was of special interest for me, given that they were the incarnation of an adventurous detective teen duo that solved crimes. General Dwight Eisenhower's *Victory in Europe* consisted of a pyramid of books that rose in the window. Farther down the avenue was the large Chrysler dealership, which in 1947 showed the Town and Country two-door coupe, with wooden siding on the doors. It was the beautiful car of my imaginings. I fantasized that my dad would buy the car and take us to the country away from the grit and grime of the city. I also daydreamed that he would buy a minia-

SOPHIA, 1937

ture version of the car, so that my brother and I could drive around in the suburbs where we would live. Such were the dreams of a nine-year-old boy. On the way home, stood the Sutherland Hotel that loomed over the corner of 47th and Drexel Boulevard, the apartment hotel where Amaryllis Hill lived.

My first stirring of romance was kindled by Amaryllis Hill, who resembled Elizabeth Taylor in the 1944 film *National Velvet*, about a young girl who saves a horse and teaches it to race. Girls and boys were about evenly divided in our 6th grade class, but the girls were more advanced developmentally, socially, and intellectually.

Betty Venturi was the class Alpha female who towered over the other girls in height and authority. When Betty inadvertently saw a picture of my mom that I carried in my wallet, she said, "Your mom looks like a movie star." She passed this judgment along to the class and almost immediately my popularity with the girls was elevated.

When Amaryllis and I crossed paths in class, on the way home, or at the Sutherland Hotel Pharmacy, she smiled and in the sweetest voice would sing, "H-i-i-i, George." And sometimes it would be "Georgie," which I did not like. I would mutter "Hi," and mutely stare at her until she broke eye contact. In class I would surreptitiously gaze at her, and my mind raced in fantasy. Nothing came of this infatuation; I was too timid to make an approach to this goddess of my dreams, but nonetheless, she always smiled and gave me a warm greeting. In my graduation signature book, she filled out two pages of greetings and warm wishes. Amy was my first awareness of an ideal woman; an image that men often carry throughout their lives. In courtly love of medieval times, the object of love was unattainable, sometimes the king's wife or a rapturously beautiful princess. For Carl Jung, psychologist, the ideal woman was part of the male collective unconscious. Later I realized that it was the idea of Amy, not the person Amy, that I loved. This was so true of my relationships with

AMARYLLIS HILL AND MERTON THAYER

women in the years to come. The imagined persona rather than the person sustained my ardor. Once the idea failed to conform to the person, sadly the bond was broken.

"Wow, Shelley, that looks so cool," I enthused. We were in Sheldon Gitelman's first floor bedroom, above my bedroom on the second floor of the 47th Street apartment building in the Kenwood district of Chicago. On Shelly's bed lay a 22-caliber chrome revolver with a pearl handle, with cartridges scattered beside the weapon, which put me in mind of Mike, our tenant, who had a revolver that he kept in his dresser and carried to work at the liquor store.

"Yeah, Vera got it for my protection from the j------ s wandering in the neighborhood. She said it was a Spanish model but hadn't fired it."

Vera was the Gitelman's' obese maid, who had some brushes with the police. Our apartment had been broken into several years previously and some coins and jewelry were taken. Dad had painted the linoleum kitchen floor before leaving on vacation, a common practice to keep the floor looking fresh. Clear imprints of a heavy woman's shoes on the sheets thrown on the floor to hide her tracks pointed to Vera's guilt. The police made inquiries but did not arrest her. Otherwise, Vera was a warm and indulgent woman who loved children, fed us cookies and milk, and each year would take Shelly and me to the Bud Billiken Parade on nearby Cottage Grove Avenue. What I learned about people from Vera is that nice people sometimes did bad things.

My second employment was short lived, but I learned much about human nature. On Cottage Grove Avenue, near our home, Good Humor Ice Cream had a warehouse filled with hand carts and bicycle carts and a large walk-in freezer containing boxes of ice cream bars, popsicles, and ice cream sandwiches. Each box held about two dozen items to be sold. Along with other young lads and adults, I showed up requesting a cart filled with ice cream to sell. "I'd like a bicycle cart," I told the manager.

Eddie, the manager, was what we would call a wise guy. With an unlit cigarette perched on his left ear, he was a glib fast talker, scheming to probe the qualities of the men and boys that came to his shop asking to peddle ice cream.

"Naw, kid you're too young. Hey, what's your name?"

"George. I'll take a hand cart,"

"Okay, here you go, Georgie boy. Take this cart. You get to keep 20% of the cash received and return any unsold goods," said Eddie.

The cart, like the others, was beat up. Eddie's business had seen better days. On my way out I stopped at home to get my brother Dave to help push the cart. We spent most of the day where many other vendors were plying their ice cream: by the 57th Street beach and at the Point, a peninsula reaching into Lake Michigan and a restricted military area where the government had set up a missile battery against a possible Soviet nuclear attack. The cold war was in full swing.

Sales were slow. On the way back to the warehouse, we stopped at a construction site, the only vendor. The construction workers came streaming to our cart. Within a few minutes we sold out the inventory. We took the empty cart back to the warehouse. Eddie was pleased. "Okay, ten bucks." He handed over eight quarters, our allotted payment. Dave and I took the money gladly and as we were leaving, Eddie surreptitiously asked, "By the way where was it that you made the score?" I described the construction site, and he said, "Good job."

The next day Dave and I pushed the cart to the construction site, and there was an adult man on a bicycle cart at the entrance. We pushed our cart up, next to his bike. "Hey kids, scram! Eddie gave me this site." Dejectedly, we moved on and tried a couple of other spots. But the business was not there. We brought the cart back with the unsold goods, now melted. We went home and tearfully told our dad that were duped into telling Eddie where we scored because he was friendly.

Dad explained, like many men in business, Eddie was out for himself and should not be trusted just because he was friendly. "Whom can you trust? he asked. We stared at him wordlessly. "Look at the person next to you, your brother, look at me, your dad; members of your family have your interest at heart, and they more than anyone can be trusted." This life lesson is so typical of the Greek mentality. Approach others with caution but trust your family wholeheartedly.

My dad took me to Sears Roebuck to buy a bike. We stood before two models of boys' bicycles with a crossbar. One was plain and blue and the other was maroon with a double lens front light and double rear lights that lit when braking, a carrier, and a buzzer horn. Dad said, "Which one do you want?" Knowing something about our family finances, that things were tight, I pointed to the blue bike while looking at the other. Dad said, "Good choice George." The bike was delivered the next day and imagine my joy when the beautiful maroon J.C. Higgins was at our doorstep. My dad said, "I had the best donkey in Kosmas. Now you have the best bike in Kenwood."

A boy on his bike signals freedom to travel. My daily summer destination was the Blackstone Library at 4904 South Lake Park Avenue that served the Kenwood and Hyde Park districts. The Blackstone Branch of the Chicago Public Library is modeled after the Erechtheion, a temple on the Athenian Acropolis, and the interior rotunda featured the themes of literature, science, labor, and art.

The library was a wonderful sanctuary from the summer heat. I would spend hours in the children's section reading on the cool mosaic tile floor. I would take out three or four children's books, tie them to my carrier, read these at home, and return the books one or two days later. My favorites were *Black Beauty* and the series on early American heroes: George Washington, Daniel Boone, Davy Crockett, Kit Carson. And the amazing Revenant legend of Hugh Glass's six-week survival in the wilderness.

The upper level of the adult section had a glass floor and stained-glass ceilings. I would peruse the books on history, geography, and art. A book on *Human Cultures* was my first encounter with antisemitism. Published in 1920, the book described Jews as an inferior race intellectually, with low IQs. Someone had circled the passage and, in the margin, and wrote, "Yeah! What about Einstein?"

My other refuge was the Museum of Science and Industry on 5700 Lake Shore Drive near the beautiful 57th Street beach. It was the only building constructed for the 1893 Columbian Exposition's "White City" that remained at that site. However, it was not until Julius Rosenwald was inspired watching his child enthralled by an interactive museum display that he resolved to finance the opening of the museum in 1933. For years, I knew the museum as the Rosenwald Museum. I was fascinated by the interactive displays of the human body and how the heart, brain, and stomach function When testing my hearing, I discovered a hearing loss in my left ear that persists to this day. The main hall had a 2000-square foot model train display, a re-creation of a 1890s town street with a nickelodeon and silent movies for five cents, displays of the inner workings of gasoline and steam engines, and a popular coal mine into which visitors could descend.

Credit must be given to Timothy Blackstone and Julius Rosenwald for their foresight in funding the library and the museum. These were places where a child on his or her own could learn about science, literature, history, geography, and art. World culture was our oyster as we devoured it through the panorama of its stories, art, places, peoples, and times. Blackstone and Rosenwald may have thought that they were merely donating buildings to house world culture, but in reality, they gave much more: a world of value and a world worth living in.

At age thirteen, I joined my dad working in an ice cream parlor and luncheonette at 16th and Blue Island, owned by Panos Kellas. We took two streetcars to get to work from 47th street. After school I would make the journey to the store on my own. It was a rough neighborhood. The store was decrepit, with stained marble tables and wire chairs in back and a busy lunch counter in front of the store, with a wide glass window featuring empty boxes of candy. Dad was the store manager.

Mr. Kellas would drive in from the suburbs in his Cadillac, a necessary trapping for a successful Greek business owner, to check out the receipts of the week. Panos Kellas opened the store just before the onset of WW II, and thanks to government restrictions on the purchase of cars and appliances, people spent extensively on ice cream, candy, and liquor. The Hubba-Hubba sundae, with three scoops of ice cream smeared with hot chocolate and fruit was a popular item, along with boxes of candy for the sweethearts of the day. As a result, candy shop owners became wealthy along with those, like Mr. Kostakis, who owned a liquor store. But times had changed and the once thriving middle class Jewish neighborhood had become African American, and the hunger for sweets abated.

On my first day working at the store, I devoured all the varieties of sundaes and banana splits and developed an aversion to sweets that persisted long afterward; I could not eat an ice cream soda or a malted milk shake for a long time. With the change in clientele, the business was barely pulling its own. Mr. Kellas offered to sell the store to my dad at favorable terns, but he declined.

Cigarettes and cigars were inexpensive and popular sale items. At the time almost all adults smoked—as well as a few children, including me. Ads showed physicians touting the health benefits of smoking in magazines and on the radio. A furtively palmed pack of Lucky Strikes or Camels would last me for a week or so. Of course, I knew smoking in front of my parents or in the house was forbidden, even without their telling me so. I would take an evening walk in the neighborhood, smoke a cigarette or two, pop a mint in my mouth to mask my cigarette breath and go home to my homework. Then a potentially life-changing event occurred.

One evening I was alone smoking a cigarette and passing Ellis Court on 47th Street. I passed an older well-built black guy walking with two girls. As I turned to go down Ellis, which was a dead-end street, one of the girls shouted, "Say, is this 47th? Yes, it is." I replied as I entered the darkened Ellis Court. Mistake. The black guy was offended. "What you yap at her for?" I continued walking down the dead-end street, and he followed me into the darkness. We had a few words and he started punching me. I punched back unevenly. We broke off contact and I ended up with a bloody nose. I headed home and entered the Sutherland Pharmacy on 47th and Drexel to buy a handkerchief to clean myself up. Shelly was at the entrance to the store. "Hey man, what happened to you?"

"I was in a fight with a black guy," I replied as I wiped the blood with a wet napkin from the counter, and we went outside. Just at that moment, the black guy with his girls turned the corner and headed north on Drexel Boulevard. I pointed him out. Shelly was inflamed. "I'm packing my rod. You wanna go after him and give him a taste of hot lead?" At that instant, I could have made a decision that would have ruined three lives, maybe more. Instead, I said, "No, I'm cool.

TALES OF THE PARK MANOR SWEET SHOP

A dream of kings
—Mark Petrakis

I n 1953, my parents purchased a luncheonette on the corner of 75th and South Park Avenue (later named Martin Luther King Drive) in Chicago for about $7000. For the residents in the neighborhood, it was more than just a place to eat: It was a space to congregate, wait for a bus, pick up non-prescription medications, purchase a newspaper or magazine, and buy boxed candy. It also functioned in summertime as the only local ice cream emporium. The Park Manor Sweet Shop came with an employee, who after several transition weeks was replaced by my parents and us children—George, David, and Peggy. We worked behind the counter along with Uncle Gus Metos, my mom's cousin, who had provided the loan for the purchase of the store.

Immigrants like my parents, Peter, and Sophia, regarded owning a retail business as the road to an independent income and some control over their family's destiny. For émigrés without an education, like my parents, self-employment was the vehicle for their children's education and their ascent into American society—hopefully, in the professions. For their children this meant no-nonsense diligence in their studies besides assisting in the store after school. After-school sports or other activities were out of the question; we were called to the store and homework once the school day ended. In a sense my family was in a space pod in an alien environment. We were the only Greek family in the Park Manor neighborhood who had a different religion, a distinct cuisine, and spoke two languages.

The store was open from early morning for breakfast to late evening, when lychnobites would come in to fill their coffee thermoses and grab a bite to eat before their night shifts began. Lunchtime was always busy as nearby factory workers clambered in for a home cooked meal costing a little over a dollar. The menu changed every day: one day it was corned beef and cabbage, the next pot roast with roasted potatoes, on another baked ham and mashed potatoes, and on Fridays fried fish and rice. All meals were cooked and served by my parents with loving care. Our family moved to a two-bedroom apartment over the store, which reduced commute time and allowed us to "be right down" when we were needed.

It was grueling, on-your-feet-all-day work, with little time for respite; it was open sixteen hours a day, seven days a week. For us children, in addition to the time spent working in the store during the school year, we devoted longer hours to helping out in the summertime. But the operation of the store depended on our parents. During the lunch rush, Uncle Gus would take cash from patrons and sell tobacco and magazines.

The neighborhood was an interesting blend of ethnicities: mainly Irish, but with a dash of Swedish, and Italian. St. Philip Neri, the local Roman Catholic Church, served the ethnic Irish and Italian families and their daughters who, along with my sister, attended Our Lady of Mercy School. The virtue of young girls was paramount in the minds of parents in the neighborhood, but when the misfortune occurred, they were nonetheless supportive.

SOPHIA KANELLIS ZIMMAR AT THE PARK MANOR SWEET SHOP, EARLY 1950S

Mary Doyle got pregnant in the back seat of Tom Haight's 1948 Hudson, a sedan with spacious interior seating. Tom was on leave from the military at the time and looking forward to the prospect of service in Korea. Once the pregnancy became apparent, marriage was discussed by the parents; but given the immaturity of the couple, the prospect of an enduring union was unlikely. Abortion was out of the question. Both parents decided that a settlement was necessary to ensure the support of the infant that Mary would raise on her own. Tom's father, Patrick, wrote a check for $1000, a considerable sum in those days. Mary, no longer in school, would appear around the neighborhood wheeling a baby carriage and surrounded by a coterie of her former teenage classmates ogling the infant; the girls, however, had no plans to follow suit outside of marriage. Mary continued to live with her parents and was loved by the Park Manor community without scorn or the stain of an unwed birth.

A dozen or so young men of the community hung out in front of or in the environs of the store, which annoyed my father no end.

Periodically, he would storm out, broom in hand, to sweep the pavement of what he considered debris, and the youth would come into the store, filling all the counter stools, and ordering a small Coke for five cents. This back-and-forth, out-and-in routine would prevail through the warm days of spring and summer, but when winter arrived the pavement was clear. As time passed, we got to know the boys individually, and since the sweet shop was their territory, they were protective of the store.

One young man had a special place in the hearts of all, Demetrios (aka Jimmy) Petas first entered the store on crutches, accompanied by a few other young men who took pains to see that he was cared for, whether he needed a ride to school or an errand to be run. Jimmy was hospitalized at age 16 for several months for the treatment of bone cancer. His leg was surgically removed below the knee, and he wore a prosthetic device during a period of remission. I would visit him at his Irish grandmother's home; his parents at the time were not on the scene. The cancer pain made life difficult and a steely bitterness pervaded Jimmy's demeanor. We did not talk about the things on the minds of young men: girls, sports, and where we were going in life. Some of our deliberations had a philosophical tone, centering on what it all means. Jimmy was not optimistic about his future. Reality hit when the cancer spread to his thigh. He had another operation to remove the cancer and was sent home, but the cancer had metastasized throughout his body. When I visited, I found him on a divan in the sunroom quietly contemplating his situation. His other friends also visited, keeping him company until the cancer finally took him away. Many of neighborhood youth attended the wake at his grandmother's home, with the corpse laid out in the dining room. All were in tears. We crammed into Jimmy's room, away from the adult mourners outside. Soon a bottle of whiskey was opened and passed around the boys and girls. Tears were replaced with mournful remembrances of Jimmy and times together, and our gathering turned into a full-fledged Irish wake to see Jimmy off.

GEORGE AT THE PARK MANOR SWEET SHOP

Meanwhile business at the Park Manor Sweet Shop was thriving. Lunch was a large revenue source for the store. The lunch crowd consisted mostly of the workers at Ryerson Engineering, an electronics firm whose main business was providing specialized antennae to the U.S. military. Across from Ryerson was the mom-and-pop Peterson Casket Company, a warehouse selling funeral supplies to local funeral homes. Marge and Leif Peterson were the elderly founders of the firm and founding members of the Swedish Club in South Shore. The owners and workers from retail stores also found their way in for lunch.

Around noon workers from the nearby factory would arrive, filling the booths and counter seats, as well as filling the air with their lively chatter. They pretty much ordered what was on the daily luncheon menu, but some would order burgers, fries, and a Coke at about half the price of the lunch meal. Mom and Dad would fill in the orders (with the help of the children in the summer) while Uncle Gus took the cash. At the end of the lunch period, my dad would take himself to a quiet corner and eat a sandwich in back of the store.

Ryerson Electronics attracted a diverse workforce of specialty workers. Some were engineers, but most were men who never thought of college and liked to work with their hands, using skills learned in their high school shop classes. With their skills training and a high school education, these men formed the base of the middle class in Chicago. They owned a home and a car and lived within easy commuting distance of work. They and their children enjoyed the expanding material comforts for their home; a television, well-made furniture, perhaps a den with a bar in the basement, and the appliances needed for home maintenance. A two-week summer vacation would bring the family together on a road trip. The workers' wives stayed at home, cared for the children, and were stewards of the household. All this because of a shop course in high school. Today, most high schools no longer offer shop classes to students. Instead, the chimera of college preparation is the norm for students who largely lack the skills or interest in higher education.

However, not all the Ryerson workers lacked an interest in things intellectual. Robert Bomce regularly ordered his usual lunch: a tuna sandwich with onion and tomato on wheat toast along with a glass of lemonade. His frame was Lincolnesque, and his Adam's apple vibrated in concert with his booming voice as he discussed his latest reading interest with workmates and anyone, myself included, who cared to listen. A devotee of Ayn Rand, he discussed her worldwide bestselling novel, *The Fountainhead,* with sincere passion. The story of an "intransigent young architect Howard Roark, whose integrity was as unyielding as granite; of Dominique Francon, the exquisitely beautiful woman who loved Roark passionately but married his worst enemy; and of the fanatic denunciation unleashed by an enraged society against a great creator." For Robert, as for Rand, the ego of the creative genius was the fountainhead of societal progress, although, that society acts to censure the creator. We might reflect today on Elon Musk, who despite tremendous success in creating several ground-breaking businesses (Pay Pal, Tesla, Space X) and literally changing the energy source of automobiles, is the object of criticism for his ideas on free speech and capitalism. Robert used the lunch period to advance the idea of capitalism, including its shortcomings, contrasting it with socialism and Rand's Objectivist philosophy to a rapt audience of co-workers.

Located as it was in a middle-class residential Chicago neighborhood, the Park Manor Sweet Shop, nonetheless attracted some sophisticated and urbane customers. William Scace, president, and CEO of a division of Thor Tools, resided near our store in a six-room brick bungalow with his parents. Bill was married to his job and had an apartment downtown near his office. Once or twice a month on weekends he visited his parents in Park Manor, his boyhood home. The garage held a complete auto workshop, along with a gleaming 1955 steel gray Mercedes-Benz that Bill was modifying to race in the Bonneville Salt Flats in Utah the following summer. This was the first year of the gull wing coupe, with doors that swung outward. A couple of times a month Bill would come to the store, pull out the current auto and science magazines—*Motor Trend, Car and Driver, Popular Science*—take a seat at the counter, and absorb every page. My interest in cars was growing, so we would spend time going over the specifications of new cars, their potential to break records from zero to sixty mph, or the speed at a quarter mile from a dead stop. We would discuss wind resistance, engine power, and design. For instance, Bill calculated that the side-view mirror of a car traveling at 100 miles an hour would draw 7 horsepower from the speed of a car. Amid the chit-chat, I served customers ice cream and helped them with non-prescription purchases, including tobacco. I believe that Bill appreciated my enthusiasm for cars and my spending evening hours at the store while my parents were resting. Progress in the modification of the Mercedes proceeded for the run to Bonneville Salt Flats for Speed Week in late August into September. At one point, he asked if I cared to join him for the run to Utah to assist in maintenance and share the driving. After a quick judgment of how my parents would respond to my traveling cross country with a customer, I declined. But not with regret. After all, I was a soda jerk, not an auto mechanic.

The promise of the Park Manor Sweet Shop paid off. Within a year, the business was on its feet, debts were paid off, loans were repaid, and improvements made that expanded the business. The following year we bought a new car. While we lived over the store in a small apartment during the first years, my parents invested in the "nifty fifties" equities market that assured their comfortable retirement later. We three children went to college in Chicago, one after the other, realizing our parents' dream as we continued to put in time at the store. The neighborhood changed from all white to all black except for our family. We continued to live over the store for a few years until we moved to the affluent South Shore district after I completed high school.

There were many other rich vignettes that crossed the threshold of the Park Manor Sweet Shop, recollections of a time and place that are etched in memory. Our Greek ancestry made us a unique strand in the Park Manor tapestry.

THREE

PARDON MY ETHNICITY, I'M GREEK, OR AM I?

Never to talk about oneself is a refined form of hypocrisy.
—Friedrich Nietzsche

At times we come face to face with our ethnicity without warning. Unlike persons of color or those with Asian features, we do not wear our background—Irish, Moldavian, Jewish, Norwegian—on our sleeves; nor is it something most of us hide. Nonetheless, we are surprised when thus confronted by a stranger asking, "Are you Greek?"

Moments before, I had settled on a park bench across from the local public library, book in hand, a refugee from home seclusion seeking a quiet place for a solitary read. Out of the corner of my eye, I watched a sprightly elderly man approach, walking his mixed breed dog. As the man came nearer, the dog ran up to me, sniffed my shoes and pants, and moved away—evidently unimpressed by the odors emitted. However, the man stopped and asked, "Are you

Greek?" Momentarily confused, I looked down at my t-shirt with its emblazoned "I Make a Difference!" Greek Orthodox Church of our Saviour in Rye, New York, specially made for wearing on the bi-annual church clean-up day, and replied, "Yes I am."

He looked at me inquiringly, "So am I; not fully, but my grandfather was Greek." My interlocutor, a man in his seventies, of small frame and a ruddy complexion, had lively eyes but not a trace of southern European ancestry. His eyes shifted back and forth as he stopped his walk, clearly intending to continue our exchange.

I asked him, "What part of Greece was your grandfather from?"

"Oh, from Ioannina," he replied.

Ioannina, the capitol of Epirus in northwestern Greece, immediately came to mind, as did Ali Pasha, the Albanian ruler who controlled the western provinces of Greece and Albania for the better part of a half century during the late Ottoman times. "Have you been to Ioannina?" I questioned. "Oh yes," my companion replied. "I was there the year before last; it's an amazing place. I visited the house where my grandfather grew up before he came to the United States. I also visited the 'Kastro.'"

The Kastro (castle) was Ali Pasha's well-fortified refuge situated in the middle of a lake. Ali Pasha had tried to establish a separate state apart from the Ottoman Sublime Porte. After the defeat of his forces, he was deceived into surrendering to the Ottoman janissaries with a promise of pardon. When told to present his head for severing, Ali proclaimed, "My head . . . will not be surrendered like the head of a slave." He was shot repeatedly, his head severed and brought to Constantinople to Ottoman Sultan Mahmud II.

"Have you been to Ioannina?" the man asked in turn. "Indeed, yes," I replied. "Ioannina is a spectacularly beautiful place, but my family is from southern Greece—Peloponnesus. "Oh," he remarked. "Nice talking with you." He ambled off, his dog picking up the pace after a period of forced restraint.

It was at Peloponnesus, during the Battle of Navarino, that the people of Greece achieved their independence from the Ottoman Empire after a bloody ten-year struggle. Ioannina remained under Ottoman control for another 80 years before Epirus was joined to Greece. My great-great-grandfather, Anagnostis Zymaras, (b. 1801) was a soldier in 1821 under Captain Kostas Katsikas and took part in all his engagements against the Ottoman forces. Anagnostis' name appeared as a combatant at the battle of Spetses, August 1824. He was listed again in 1826 as a member of a battalion from Arcadia. Greece had achieved its independence as a nation and Greeks their identity in the modern world.

SOPHIA AND GEORGE, 1939

On the cusp of liberation, Anagnostis married and had three children—Athanasios (b. 1828), Sofia (b. 1830), and Pagona. (b. 1832). A man of substance, Anagnostis was best man at the wedding of Giorgios Kostakis of Tsitalia and Theodora Hontzas on July 1, 1845, in Kosmas.

When I say I am Greek, what does this mean? On one level, it means my mother and mother tongue were Greek. It is through one's mother that primary language, personal identity, and family bonds are formed. We turn to our mother for love and learn to love through her tender care. In many cultures, ethnic identity is transmitted through the maternal line. My mother and father married 30 years after his arrival in the United States, and I was born in the same year. My mom was quite young and quite beautiful, and I was always at her side.

On another level, our Greekness is reflected in our DNA. The human genome knows nothing of national boundaries or cultural diversity, but DNA travels to every corner of the globe. The migration of folks is a tapestry of where people have been and an image of their stay at different regions of the planet. On my birthday, I was gifted with an Ancestry Profile Kit. Some spittle into a tube, and my DNA profile was available after a three-week wait.

What did the profile reveal? Going deeply into the past, most of my DNA reflected the southern part of Europe, mostly the Italian peninsula. Moving forward in time, the region of Georgia in southern Russia was in evidence. Moreover, there was a trace of Jewish DNA. However, in the 19th century the DNA was concentrated in southern Greece, specifically Peloponnesus.

At the turn of the 20th century, three bands of my DNA traveled from the Sparta region to New York, Boston, and Chicago, where my father had settled in the United States. He was within the band that landed in Chicago in 1907. Shortly after my profile was made available, I received an email from a Nicki Platt, whose grandmother was from the same part of Greece and claimed to be related to me.

As it turned out, after checking with my sister Peggy, I learned that we were indeed second cousins to the Kilavos family. Nikki's grandmother, Lygeri Athanasiou Zoumaras Kilavos (1857–1944), was my paternal grandfather's sister. While Greek was not written on my DNA as such, nonetheless, both my mother's and father's families lived within 10 miles of each other through the entire 19th century.

Trolling through my dad's family records, we found that Panayiotis Gioryios Zoumaras (1888–1986) was born in the Kynouria district of Kosmas or Vrondama, which were nearby villages in Peloponnesus. Residents of these villages had dual residences; they typically summered in cool, mountainous Kosmas and spent their winters in warmer Vrondama. Kosmas is in Arcadia and Vrondama in Laconia, a few kilometers from my mother's home village, Geraki (or the ancient Gerakion). The Arcadians were mentioned in Homer's *Iliad* as having been given 60 ships by Agamemnon to join his forces in the war against Troy. The Laconians were centered in Sparta.

My grandfather, Gioryios Athanasios-Chantzi (honorific for a Greek pilgrim who traveled to Jerusalem and prayed at Christ's tomb) Zoumaras (1855–1944). A farmer with properties scattered between his residences in Kosmas and Vrondama, Gioryios married Panayiota Dimitriou Karkas (1862–1936). His father, Athanasios Anagnostis Zoumaras (b. 1828), who married Aikaterini Maroudas (1844-1910), was the son of Anagnostis Zymaras. Gioryios along with the other residents of Kosmas, would carve out strips of pine wood to fashion the teeth of looms. The comb-like reeds separated the warp thread. Men from Kosmas would carry prepared reeds and unfinished pine strips to distant villages to make repairs on looms. Gioryios traveled with his son Panayiotis (my father), who was skilled at reed carving, to distant parts of mainland Greece and the Ottoman-occupied areas to repair looms.

Northern Greece—part of the Ottoman Empire, with Salonika as the district center—did not achieve independence until 1912. Toward the end of the 19th century, Kemal Ataturk's father was the customs officer of Macedonia in Salonika. A military pass dated March 20, 1900 revealed that my grandfather, Gioryios, traveled from Adrianople to Constantinople on March 23. On the document, grandfather was described as being of medium stature, aged 45, with chestnut eyes and a proportionate mouth (which means that the mouth corresponds to facial features). In Kosmas, he was known as "verryios," or tall as a pine tree. He was active in the purchase and selling of real estate in Kosmas and Vrondama. Gioryios' father—my great grandfather, Athanasios Anagnosti Zoumaras—was born in Kosmas in 1828 and was married to Panayiota Dimitriou Rorris.

My father, Panayiotis Gioryios Zoumaras, disembarked in New York in 1907. Upon arrival, he traveled to Chicago, living with his uncle Constantinos "Gus" Zumaras (1869–1936), a bookkeeper who was married to Claudia Zumaras, an American woman; they had a son named Stanley Zumaras. Gus's brother, Ioannis "Joseph" Athanasiou Zumaras (1876-1915) was married to Anna Pulaski Zumaras (1884-1970). The brothers had opened the Zumaras Bros. Candy Store prior to 1900 at 287–89 Noble Street, which was an ongoing enterprise until Joseph's untimely death of pneumonia in 1915. No doubt my father learned the confectioner's craft at the mentoring guidance of his uncle Joseph.

Panayiotis worked briefly as a carpenter's assistant in the South Chicago steel mills. Later he sent for his brother, Thomas, (Athanasios,1893–1985), and they went into partnership with their first cousins, the Delyiannis brothers, in several successful confectioneries, a movie theater, and real estate ventures. My father became a master confectioner, which he remained for much of his life. To Americanize, he took the name Peter Zimmar (Zymaras) and retained this name through the remainder of his life. Dad, his brother, and partners the Delyiannis brothers went big into real estate, movie theaters and several sweet shops. With the first World War and the roaring twenties that followed, the money rolled in. Dad was also heavily into equities. These men, without wives or family, lived frugally, often at the

PASSPORT, GIORYIOS ZOUMARAS, 1900

back of their businesses, like Silas Mariner accumulated wealth and on occasion would splurge.

In 1924, Peter returned to Europe onboard a liner, sitting at the first-class dinner table with his fellow passenger J.P. Morgan II. Such a dramatic status change came about thanks to rapid wealth accumulation in the equities market. Dad presciently bailed out before the Crash of '29, but then lost his pile with the bank collapse of 1932. From Paris, Peter traveled to Greece to arrange for the passage of his sister to the United States. He returned to the United States and opened a confectionery next to Chicago's Biograph Theater, later made famous by the assassination of John Dillinger by Federal agents. My father recalled that Dillinger came to the store for ice cream that summer. My dad worked with his hands for much of his life—as a boy making the delicate wood combs that threaded fibers in looms and as a carpenter in the Chicago steel mills before joining his uncles Gus and Joseph at their candy store on Noble Avenue. As Joseph's apprentice, Peter mastered the art of making candy creations of light or dark chocolate, fudge, or the varieties of caramel. His chocolate creams were perfectly shaped and almost identical in appearance. He combined chocolate with walnuts and caramel to create so-called turtle candies. Easter, Mother's Day, and Valentine's Day were especially high-volume periods for candy makers. Peter spent much of his working life making varieties of chocolate candies for his own businesses or working for other candy shops. Eventually, he brought his sister Stella into the candy store by the Biograph Theater.

For many years while I was growing up, my dad was someone's employee, often as a candy maker in a confectionery shop. At times he was a short-order cook or would make ice cream. His wife, Sophia, gave birth to me in 1937, brother Adamianos (David) in 1940, and Panagiota (Peggy) in 1943. Even with the blessings of a family,

PETER, 1936

my dad's life was hard. He would leave for work at midday and return late at night. I recall that he used the earlier carpentry skills he had acquired when he made a beautiful wooden lay-out table for our Lionel electric train, which he fashioned with tracks and roads and a wayside for a train station.

Along with his family responsibilities and work, my dad had a major illness that almost killed him when we children were very young. Apparently, for several months, dad was suffering from excruciating pain in the upper abdomen. So great was the agony that he would lie on the floor for relief. The diagnosis was cancer and the prognosis fatal. We were all in the doctor's office when this call was made. We children were not told anything but felt the terror of the moment. After leaving the office in tears, we were on the way down a flight of stairs when my mother said, "Let's go to this doctor," as she stared at the office door of another physician.

In the office, the doctor made a quick evaluation, and said, "We need to take you to the hospital immediately for surgery." The surgery forthwith revealed not cancer, but a bag of gall bladder stones so numerous that it was a medical record at the time. This illness and the long recovery set my dad back because he could not work for several months. We were poor, but never felt poverty.

Dad had a fourth grade education, but he was an avid reader of books and newspapers. He had a good comprehension of Greek history, but he also read about other areas of politics and culture. I cannot remember discussing his learning or his political beliefs with him. He was a Roosevelt Democrat but cared little for the claims of politicians. At one July 4th parade, I recall that he commented that the marching Chicago machine politicians were much like the Bolshevik minions that marched in Russia, a kind of equivalency of political orders. In discussions with male relatives and visitors to our home, he would state his position frankly, without ardor or compromise.

In 1953, the fortunes of our family changed when my parents purchased the Park Manor Sweet Shop, a luncheonette that they expanded into a confectionery and ice cream emporium. The store also sold toiletries, dry goods, tobacco, newspapers, magazines, and non-prescription medicines—a drug store without a druggist. It was suggested that if I studied pharmacy, the circle would be closed, and prescriptions would fill out the financial plan for the store. The store came with an employee, but it soon became a family business, with my parents as co-owners and myself, Dave, and Peggy as staff. But the bulk of work fell on my parents. We moved to the apartment over the store and very quickly were a presence in the neighborhood, which was changing from Irish Catholic to African American.

So here we were, Greeks among the Blacks at a time when African American consciousness was emerging to political action. Our connection to Greekness was through the St. Constantine and Helen Greek Orthodox Church. Thanks to my mother's deep faith, incense burned for morning or evening prayers before the household icons, with church attendance every Sunday. Regular attendance at worship services ingrained in me both the Orthodox faith and Greek ethnicity. Hellenic School met weekday afternoons and eventually became K–8 grade school. The school was staffed by high-level educators—for instance, Andrew Kopan (1924–2006), later professor and chair of education at DePaul University in Chicago.

Three days a week, my brother and I boarded a streetcar that would take us from 47th and Drexel Boulevard to 74th and Stony Island, a ride of about 30 minutes through several neighborhoods—Hyde Park and University of Chicago, South Shore, and finally to the Koraes school. [Adamantios Koraes (1748–1833) was a Greek humanist scholar whose advocacy of revived classicism laid the foundations for the Greek struggle for independence.] We had a 20-minute pre-school recess period and reluctantly pressed into school from 4:00 to 6:00 pm three days a week. Since my mother spoke only Greek to me as an infant and toddler, my accent was not a cacophony to the ears of Greek teachers.

In large and small ways, both conscious and unconscious, we students were transformed and connected to the very idea of what it means to be Greek in a world where Greek is not spoken, where Greece is not a superpower, and where Hellenism is a topic in history no longer read. What profit can there be in such study of Greek? What makes such study profound? Simply stated, another language, another voice, another culture, another pair of eyes, another way of thinking, another soul. It becomes a matter of identity, who we are, and what of us we preserve. We live in a culture in which for many their identity is based on race, social class, or ethnicity; but for Greeks it is something more.

The sexes were segregated in class, with good learning taking place on the girl's side of the classroom and disruptions to teaching on the boy's side. The instruction was mainly in language, reading, and writing. We were asked to read out loud, learn poems, mostly about the Greek Revolution, and write short essays. Once a year on March 25th, my brother and I were hustled onto the streetcar dressed in borrowed Evzone costumes, fezzes, and slippers with pom poms, to the amusement of our fellow passengers. At church, we recited poems on the heroism of Greeks striving for independence, the treachery of Turks sustaining the yoke of slavery, and the Holy Spirit inspiring the quest for freedom. Each of us went to the stage and in a single breath recited a long poem on the cause of the Greeks to a beaming parental audience. Some of the friendships I made at Greek School fell by the wayside as we attended different high schools and began the process of drifting away from the embrace of the Holy Church.

The Sons of Pericles and Daughters of Penelope, social clubs for Greek Orthodox Church Youth of America (GOYA) programs under the stewardship of Fr. Basil Gregory (1925–2001), invited teenagers to participate in youth activities such as basketball, soccer, and dancing. Our purpose there was to meet and mingle with other youngsters of Greek descent. Fellowship and sports activities were the reason given for GOYA, but boys and girls were looking to meet kindred souls for friendship and some tentative touch with romance. In our Greek households, marriage with a Greek was preferred, often strongly. GOYA for teens became a meeting milieu for Orthodox youth.

In my case, a chance meeting at GOYA with an older teen provided me with a role model. Jim Kostas, a high school senior, had just been admitted to Northwestern University. I was a high school first-year student. Jim dressed smartly in preppy fashion, smoked cigarettes, spoke in a sophisticated manner, and highlighted the importance of a college education to life success. Jim also looked beyond our parochial Greek social culture toward finding a place in the broader American culture. Coincidentally, after completing our education at different colleges and establishing different careers, both Jim and I left Chicago and married Greek American women; in addition, we each had a son and daughter, served on the church parish council together, and ended up with homes in Westchester County, New York a few miles from each other. We maintained a respectful but reserved friendship. However, I am ever grateful to Jim for his counsel at that critical period of my life.

The GOYA bonds carried over to our college years and became lifelong friendships. My friends George and Nick Panagakis, Gus Alevizos, Jim Boves, Mike Simos, and my brother David were at the core of my social life. Most of us entered the Chicago Campus of the University of Illinois and by fits and starts completed our undergraduate work at Roosevelt University, named after Franklin and Eleanor for their endeavors in human rights. The most significant course during my years in college was the Great Books course, starting with Homer's *Iliad* and working through the profound literature of Europe. The course cultivated a sensibility for art, philosophy, and the humanities and an appreciation of the contributions of Hellenism to world culture.

For young Greek men and women, another social was the Hellenic University Club, which drew Greek youth from all parts of Chicago, mainly to socialize and make contact for potential romance.

Gradually these associations held less sway over me as I focused on my psychology studies as a research assistant in the psychiatry department of Northwestern's medical school. I stayed on at Roosevelt for a master's degree in psychology and pushed off to the University of Buffalo for a doctorate in experimental psychology.

My parents were uncertain about my doing graduate work in psychology. In my mother's mind, it was not medicine, law, or pharmacy (that dream had long died). On the other hand, the significance of education was firmly embedded in Sophia's mind. An elementary school counselor had recommended that perhaps a technical high school would be better for me than an academic high school like Hyde Park, which was a top school in Chicago. Perhaps I would be more comfortable training as an electrician or an auto mechanic, the counselor suggested. Actually, at the time and a little later, I did work in a garage, but mainly serving customers for gas rather than fixing cars. My mother said, "He needs to go to a college school." Like some immigrants, both my mom and dad regarded education as a must for advancement.

My mom would sit and work with us on our mathematics homework. As a girl, she was forced out of school at grade six because girls in Greece did not go to gymnasium (high school). They worked in the household and prepared their trousseau for marriage. Learning was that missing element in mom's life, and she would not deny education to any of her children, male or female. So, I was admitted to Hyde Park High School; during the first year I absorbed George Eliot's *Silas Mariner*, the second year Stephen Crane's *The Red Badge of Courage*, the third year Ernest Hemingway's *For Whom the Bell Tolls*, and fourth year Walt Whitman's *Leaves of Grass*.

At the University of Buffalo (later SUNY at Buffalo) graduate program, I engaged for the first time in an environment that was without family or Greeks. The Buffalo community was largely immigrant and Roman Catholic, but the university attracted students and professors from around the United States. I settled into my studies and new friendships. I sought to make contact and attend services at an Orthodox Church. A philosophy professor at the University was an acolyte of the American Orthodox Church and invited me to worship services, which were held in the living room of his home. I attended Divine Liturgy several times but found the liturgy in English somewhat disconcerting, so stopped attending services. Ethnicity trumped Orthodoxy. However, I was of two minds about moving away from church and family and moving toward the broader American culture and new attachments.

Immigrants and, to lesser degree, the children of immigrants confront a challenge to their identity: Does one adopt the majority culture and seek positive relations with the culture, or does one maintain one's original cultural identity and avoid relations with the dominant culture? Traditionally, most, but not all, immigrants and their children adopt the former approach and reject the latter; they assimilate. They drop their language and adopt the language and cultural norms of the dominant culture. This was characteristic of Europeans who immigrated to the United States at the time my dad, Peter, did. Other immigrants avoid relations with the dominant culture but maintain their original cultural identity; they separated. The Hasidim of eastern Europe follow this approach and maintain their religion, language (Yiddish), and cultural practices in separate enclaves. A third approach is to adapt to the dominant culture and maintain identity with the old culture; they integrate. To an extent, my dad, Peter, integrated. He anglicized his name, spoke English at home, and had business relations with Americans. However, his social contacts were with family and other Greeks. Integration had limits for my parents and that included whom we would marry.

I had not been home in two years. Toward the end of my doctoral work, my brother David came to Buffalo, moved in with me, and, in the process, his presence drew me back to my roots. My personal life was in conflict. I was on a life course with an outsider, marriage to whom would have confused my parents. Not that they would have rejected anyone that I brought home; they were loving people. Nonetheless, we had expectations of each other. Dave's counsel led to a gradual change in course.

Dave and I attended the AHEPA (American Hellenic Educational and Progressive Association) national convention in Toronto. Founded in 1922, AHEPA worked tirelessly to protect the civil rights of Greek Americans. It evolved into an educational and philanthropic organization of 400 chapters and held a bi-annual national conference. My sister and parents arrived from Chicago, and it was great to see them, conflicted though I was. My college friends had also made the trip. A wave of nostalgia for things Greek overcame me. The convention itself was a boozy event with youthful banter and camaraderie. It was a contrast to a rather austere academic life and the demands of a complicated relationship. Such were my concerns as we departed Toronto.

My family and I clambered into my sister's sedan and made our way to the US border at Niagara Falls, New York. As we approached the entrance gate, we realized that neither parent had their passport nor evidence of US citizenship. We faced hours of interrogation and perhaps arrest. The border guard came up to the car, scanned our smiling faces and focused immediately on Dad, the apparent undocumented immigrant. "Where were you born?" he queried? Panayiotis Zoumaras of Kosmas, became Peter Zimmar, citizen of the United States of America, looked the border agent square in the face, and said in a clear voice, "Chicago." "Move on" the agent said in disbelief.

So, what is ethnicity? The bond between mother and the mother tongue is key to ethnic identity. The passing down of customs, tradi-

PEGGY, DAVID, SOPHIA, AND PETER, C. 1963

tions, and language of a people is mainly the duty of the mother and less of the father. Once an infant is born, it stays with the mother. The first words it hears and picks up are from the mother. Moreover, the bonds of family and love of family is transmitted through mother—the woman that providence has brought to your side, the mother of your children. This is the foundation of ethnicity.

We no longer speak of races but of ancestral populations, which fall roughly into Africa, Asia, Europe, and the Mediterranean region—southern Europe and Mesopotamia (now the Middle East). Rhinoplasty surgeons differentiate the noses of each region. For instance, Mediterraneans tend to have noses with a hump in the region between the tip and forehead and a slightly drooping tip, whereas people from north Europe have wide-base noses and protruding tips, while those native to northwest Europe have pointing-up noses. In general, European people have slightly wider and longer noses compared to other ethnic groups in the world. The genomes of human groupings also reveal differences in health, cognition, and personality.

Greeks not only have distinctive noses, but their identity is tied to their ancestral history.

Within the Mediterranean ancestral populations, Greeks claim connection to the Hellenes of antiquity—those people of brilliance who blazed into human consciousness. Theirs is a profound identity: namely, that our Greek DNA is connected to the souls who created philosophy; established science; founded arts, theater, and literature; and brought the teachings of Christ to the world through the Holy Scriptures. Whether or not we can boast of Greek ethnicity, Grecian identity is a universal imbued in what psychoanalyst Carl Jung calls the collective unconscious of mankind. As Greeks we carry that identity into the world and, hopefully, make it a better place to live.

Curiosity about the origins of our identity often carries us to our geographic roots. We seek the places where our parents were born, went to school, formed friendships, and grew to become adults. In my case my ancestors were in Laconia.

FOUR

PILGRIMAGE TO LACONIA

The boat is safer anchored at the port,
but that is not the aim of boats.
—Paolo Coelho

When we think of a pilgrimage, like Chaucer's *Canterbury Tales*, a spiritual journey comes to mind. My grandfather, Gioryios Zymaras (Zoumaras), made a pilgrimage to Jerusalem in 1900, where he prayed before the tomb of Christ and earned the right to attach *Hadji* to his surname. Hadji is probably taken from the practice of Moslems of making a pilgrimage to Mecca, a Hadj. My pilgrimage to Laconia was to pay tribute to the places where my parents, Panayiotis (Peter) and Sophia, were born and grew up—a pilgrimage to one's origins.

I made the trip to my mother's village for the first time with my sister, Peggy, and our first cousin, Phalia. We drove in my 1966 Volvo from Athens to the plains of Sparti. This was years before the National Highway that tunneled through the mountains was built, so the trip took six hours of bruising hairpin turns though Northern

Peloponnesus that tossed my passengers from side to side. We arrived late afternoon in Sparti, somewhat shaken.

My mother's lineage can be traced to the killing in Ottoman times of a Turk in the village of Bertzovas (now Partheni) near Tripoli. Four Kanellis brothers split for different parts of Peloponnesus to avoid capture: two to Geraki, one to Gouves, and another to Zaganou. Years before, the childless wife of the Kanellis ancestral forebear, instructed her husband on her deathbed to marry the young gypsy servant tending her. The apocryphal family narrative is that the Kanellis line, which included the four brothers, issued from this union.

Years later, a descendant, Athanasios Panagiotis Kanellis (1836–1905), married Aikaterini Adamatiou Maroudas (1844–1910) in Geraki; their son, Diamandis Athanasiou Kanellis (1870–1951) was to be my maternal grandfather. He married Garyfalia Doulfas (1884-1966), the daughter of priest Mihalis Doulfopoulos, in 1902. They had eight children—my precious aunts, uncles, and my mother, Sophia. Diamantis was a substantial landowner, respected mayor, and godfather

ADIAMANTIS KANELLIS, LEFT OF PRIEST, AND FAMILY

to many children in Geraki and surrounding villages. After the villagers of Geraki had turned over the annual olive crop to a flimflam exporter who ran off with the receipts of the olive sale, Diamantis reimbursed every family for their loss, Such civic duty typifies the Kanellis family.

While in Greece, my sister and I visited with my mother's brothers and sisters, our beautiful and loving aunts and uncles, and got to know our Kanellis cousins. From Sparti, we traveled 40km to the spacious home in Geraki built in 1900 by Adiamantis Kanellis. Uncle Mihalis, mom's brother, was caring for my dad's properties. We decided to go to Kosmas to see where my father's ancestors—Anagnostis, Athanasios, Gioryios, and my dad, Panayiotis—had set down their roots. None of the Zymaras clan lived in Kosmas or Vrondama, and their homes were vacant. However, my paternal grandmother's descendants, the Karkas family, were still living in Kosmas. We piled into the Volvo—Uncle Mihalis, his daughters Phalia and Mando, cousin Phalia, son Diamandis, and my sister Peggy. Uncle Mihalis

ADIAMANTIS KANELLIS HOME, GERAKI, LACONIA

KARKAS MOTHER, STELIOS, PEGGY, DIAMANTES, MANDO,
PHALIA, GARIFALIO, AND MIHALIS IN KOSMAS, ARCADIA, 1966

questioned why in the world I would buy a two-door passenger car when four doors were available. Was it a matter of cost? This was a question raised by all my Greek relatives. I believe this query speaks to the contrast between how Americans and Greeks relate to their cars. In the United States style and size matter, whereas in Greece and Europe, economy and convenience of passengers are sought. For Americans, appearance takes precedence over the comfort of fellow travelers. A sleek, sporty two-door is preferred over a cumbrous and clunky four-door sedan that offers the well-being and felicity of the passengers. The four girls were cramped in the back seat of the Volvo, with me, Uncle Mihalis, and Diamantes on his lap in front as off we went up the craggy, rock-strewn road to the beautiful village of Kosmas.

Kosmas lies in the mountains of Arkadia on Mount Parnon. Surrounded by forests of chestnut and pine trees, it is high enough for there to be a difference in temperature of ten or more degrees from Tripoli, Sparta, Leonideon, and the east coast of the Peloponnesus,

PLATEIA KOSMAS

which are about an hour away. In the summer Kosmas is cool, and in the winter, it is so cold that residents go south to their homes in Vrondama. The village is set near the top of Mount Parnon, and from my father's house, one could glimpse the Myrtoan Sea and the Isle of Spetses.

The nearby plateia is one the most beautiful village squares in Greece, with wide-spreading plane trees shading the entire square. The Lion Fountain of Kosmas splashes cold and clear mountain water throughout the summer months. We escaped the hot summer sun of Laconia at my father's house.

Located on the road from Leonideon and near the plateia, the house had two floors, with the ground level for storage and for the animals to provide their body heat in winter for the occupants above. Upstairs included a fireplace (*dzakei*) and rooms for sleeping and woodworking. We explored the property, and Diamantis found a *hteni* (he is holding it in the photo), which for many years was the main product of the Kosmites.

A hteni is the reed on a loom through which the fibers pass to make cloth. It is made of pine strips and smoothed so that the fibers pass through the needle undamaged. Kosmites spent the winter months stripping pine to fashion htenai. In the spring, they traveled to towns in Greece and the Ottoman regions and repaired standing looms with the parts for making htenai they had accumulated over the winter. Grandfather Gioryios and dad, as a boy, supplemented their income with such toil far from Kosmas. As strangers (*xenai*) in different locales, the Kosmites had developed a dialect for communication among themselves. For instance, coffee was *moudzo* and young woman *poula*. Much of the dialect and the skill for making htenai passed from memory when my father left Kosmas for the United States, but his capacity for hard work remained.

I felt close to the picturesque Kosmas and to my father's roots in Arkadia. However, my mother's village, Geraki, was home, with loving family—uncles, aunts, and cousins. My physiognomy resembled the maternal side more than paternal, and they treated me as one of

GIORYIOS ZYMARAS'S HOME, KOSMAS, ARKADI

54

theirs. We clambered back into the car, leaving the cool Kosmas for the warmth of Geraki.

Along the way from Kosmas to Geraki, we encountered a roadside pavilion with a blaze of blue and white fluttering Greek flags, a memorial ceremony of the WWII resistance to the Nazis. Politicians and representatives of resistance groups were on a dais before a scattered audience. Reminded of having lived through the brutality of the period, Uncle Michael, with tears in his eyes, suggested that we move on to our destination.

DAVID, PEGGY AND GEORGE
BUCKINGHAM FOUNTAIN, (C.1946)

FIVE

HAMARTIA: MISSING THE MARK

. . . for all have sinned and fall short of the glory of God
—Romans, 3,23

S hortly after WWII ended, Greek immigration to the United
States reopened, especially to those without communist sympa-
thies. After Winston Churchill's March 5, 1946, Iron Curtain
speech at Westminster College, U.S. attitudes toward the Soviet Union hardened and the ally against fascism became an enemy
against freedom. My dad's cousin Christos Cheronis was an early
arrival (in 1946), and for brief periods he stayed at our home as he
applied for investiture of his credentials in medicine. A tall, handsome man in his mid-40s with an aquiline nose and pencil mustache,
he cut a dashing figure. Yet a shroud of doom encircled his persona.

Christos was a physician, and during the war of occupation
against the Nazis a resistance (antartes) leader in Peloponnesus operating out of his and my dad's home village, Kosmas. Like many in-
tellectuals of the day, Christos's politics were left of center. My dad's
family expressed points of view that stood in sharp divergence to my

mom's family, which had a traditional and conservative outlook on politics and life. In a sense these opposing views may account for the split personality that I at times feel myself while embracing contradictory ideas.

Christos's troop roamed Laconia and Arcadia unimpeded. While posters for information leading to his capture were posted throughout the region, he would enter Sparta without his band of brothers, obtain medical supplies from a fellow physician, Dr. Anarghios Kanellis (a relative of my mother), and have lunch with him and his Austrian wife, Gisela,[1] without fear of capture. Gisela cautioned Christos not to kill Germans; the retaliation on the populace would be brutal.

Early in the resistance, a company of Italian troops was sent to the redoubt Christos had in Kosmas to burn the village. Previously, while in Geraki, my mother's village, the Italian captain had brought all the villagers to the plateia (town square) and harangued them about their silence on Christos's whereabouts. Yet none came forward. In disgust, the captain sputtered in Greek, "Tha pao Kosmas, kapso Kosmas; tha pao Geraki, kapso Geraki. I will go to Kosmas and burn it to the ground; I will return to Geraki and burn it to the ground."

The mountain roads to Kosmas were little more than sharp, rocky footpaths, wide enough perhaps for a donkey cart. A traveler would proceed up the steep grade to a point and swing upward in the opposite direction to the next high point, much as a sailboat tacking in the water. The Italian company proceeded in single file when suddenly gunfire from across the valley struck the men one after the other. Captain Cheronis's troop fired mercilessly on the hapless Italians. Moreover, their retreat was blocked by partisans in hidden positions on the road below. A few Italians made it back to Geraki and were hidden by the villagers from reprisal by both the partisans and the German commandant in charge of the region.

The year Christos arrived in the U.S.; Christmas was celebrated at our apartment. Christmas at our home was truly a festive affair. A large pine tree that was as tall as the ceiling was overly laden with ornaments and stringy silver strands that hid the branches. On Christmas morning, gifts mysteriously appeared under the tree that had been bare the night before. One year I stayed up in the front room to wait for Santa Claus. After hearing bells and the clop-clop of a horse from the street below, I looked outside to see the milkman making his rounds in what was no doubt one of the last horse-drawn milk wagons. I fell asleep and when I woke to the gift-laden tree, my faith in Santa remained unbroken.

Dad's brother, Athanasios (Tom), sister, Styliani (Stella) and families arrived on Christmas day, as did mom's cousins Tom and Gus Metos. We filed around the dining room table, and Christos was placed at its head, being the luminary that he was. The conversation centered on the civil war in Greece (1943–1949), with some taking the Greek government's side, which was supported by Britain and the United States, while others took the side of the KKE (Kommounistikó Kómma Elládas), a Marxist–Leninist political party in Greece supported by communists in Bulgaria. In Yalta, Stalin had accepted that Greece would remain in the West's sphere of influence and so withdrew the agents that were in Greece during the war. Nonetheless, the communists fought on and were defeated in 1949, with the remnant fleeing to Eastern bloc countries. Being the man of few words that he was, Christos engaged little in the conversation, but somehow his presence dominated the room.

After the guests left, Christos spent a few days at our home until he established his residency at the hospital. Gleefully, I brandished my gift pistol with a suction cup missile in the barrel. Christos motioned for me to give him the toy gun. The bullseye target was tacked onto the mantel over the fireplace. He took the toy, extended his arm, and for what seemed the longest time took aim, then squeezed the trigger. The missile flew across the room and popped onto the very center of the bullseye. He said not a word but handed back the toy with a message in his world-weary eyes: If you aim for something, do not miss the mark; it can be tragic.

CHRISTOS CHERONIS AND PETER ZIMMAR, 1947

Hamartia, the Greek word for sin or error in judgment, conveys the idea of missing the mark. "Thus, Hamartia is an error or miscalculation, but the error may arise from any of the three ways: It may arise from 'ignorance of some fact or circumstance', or secondly, it may arise from hasty or careless view of the special case, or thirdly, it may be an error voluntary, but not deliberate, as acts committed in anger."[2] In *Aristotle's Poetics* (translated by S.H. Butcher), hamartia conveys all three meanings, and the tragic hero often falls to his doom as a result.

In the Greek tragedy "Oedipus, the King," based on myth, Oedipus commits all three errors. On the road to Thebes, he angrily encounters and unknowingly kills Laius, his father. After solving the

Riddle of the Sphinx, he enters Thebes in glory but was ignorant that Jocasta, the widowed queen he was to marry, was in fact his mother. Later, when Thebes was beset with drought and pestilence, Oedipus received omens that perhaps he was the son of Laius and that Jocasta was his mother. Oedipus's tragedy was that he both believed and disbelieved his personal situation, failed to act, and set himself up for a tragic end. In the process, he missed the mark.

When Christos contemplated the warning of Gisela about reprisals, he was of two minds. The Germans had not committed atrocities in his region of combat (Arcadia and Laconia), but carnage had taken place in other regions of Greece, notably Crete. Italy had signed an armistice with the Allies, so the Italian troops in Peloponnesus were no longer a factor in the conflict; however, the Germans moved into their encampments. So, it was entirely possible, even with a price on his head because of wiping out the Italian company, that his region would be spared.

It was not to be. A German commander traveling with his bodyguard to Tripoli in Arcadia was ambushed by an antartes band. Immediately, German command ordered that Laconia and Arcadia be cleared of antartes. From November 1943 until the Germans retreated from Greece in late 1944, the populace in the area was butchered.[3] The antartes, protected in their mountain strongholds, remained relatively unharmed by the German order to clear the area, but women were raped, the populace murdered, and villages were set in flames.

Christos both believed and did not believe that the Germans would slaughter men, women, and children in the villages that were his homeland. He both believed and did not believe that his region would be spared. Gisela had informed him of the certain German response; yet, like Oedipus, Christos clung to the hope that calamity would not strike. Like Oedipus, Christos missed the mark. For Aristotle, the tragic hero had to be a noble person of eminence, perhaps so that the fall from grace would be steep and deep. "Hamartia is an error, or a series of errors, 'whether morally culpable or not,' committed by an otherwise noble person, and these errors drive him to his doom. The tragic irony lies in the fact that a hero may err mistakenly without any evil intention, yet he is doomed no less than immorals who sin consciously. He has Hamartia and as a result his very virtues hurry him to his ruin." The ironic tragedy of noble Christos is that as a physician, he committed to both saving life and taking life and thereby bore Hamartia. While there is no word in English that denotes the meaning of hamartia, what can we take from the idea that relates to our personal behavior as we aim to negotiate our fast-changing world with our noble aspirations?

REFERENCES

1. Gizela Dusek was born in Vienna, Austria, around 1900. In 2017, she became one of the main characters of Stavroula Samailidou-Vakou's novel "Aroma Rezentas."

2. Aristotle's concept of ideal tragic hero (2022). Hamartia. http://engliterarium.com/aristotles-concept-of-ideal-tragic-hero-hamartia/

3. Greek Holocausts. The monstrous crimes of the Germans during the first occupation of Greece. http://thehistoryofgreece.blogspot.com/p/blog-page_1206.html (Google)

    November 1943: Germans kill 118 people in the village of Monodendri in Laconia. Of the 118 executed, 89 were Spartans. There were minor children and a woman among the victims.

    December 5, 1943: Germans abduct 50 prisoners from Tripoli camp. They were hanged for "exemplification" at the Andritsos Argos train station.

    December 7, 1943: Germans execute 40 hostages in prison in Gythio Laconia.

December 1943: The Germans execute a total of 119 people in the Laconia Prefecture in the villages of Andritsa, Passava, and elsewhere.

January 1944: The Germans execute 456 hostages from the prisons in Tripoli.

February 24, 1944: The Germans execute 204 people in Megalopolis, Arcadia (from the prisons in Tripoli).

March–Summer 1944: Germans kill 50 people in the village of Monodendri, Laconia in March; 244 people in Sparta in March–April; 40 people around Agios Dimitrios Zoupaina and the Sustiani region (Laconia) in June; 77 people in Panitsa, Skamnaki and Gythio in summer.

SIX

HYDE PARK

The course of a river is almost always disapproved of by its source.
—Jean Cocteau

L ocated at 62nd and South Stony Island Avenue, Hyde Park
High School stood as a premier secondary school in Chicago.
In my four years in attendance, the school was first in the state
Latin contest, first in the city math contests, first in debate, and
first in the city chess competition. Its purview extended into poorer
sections near Cottage Grove and the affluent sections of Kenwood
and South Shore. We were truly a diverse, but cosmopolitan, as-
semblage of students and faculty. Over half of the school's graduates
were admitted to college, while the city and national average was
5%. The academic influence of the University of Chicago hovered
nearby, and many of my classmates were the daughters and sons of
U of C professors.

Attending a high-performance school like Hyde Park is chal-
lenging—and humbling. Certainly, it's more difficult to succeed
alongside intellectually more gifted students than yourself. Yet the
setting was such that it buzzed with a creative and cerebral fervor.
Our achievement-crammed class motto was *Strive for a high goal and*

when you achieve it strive for a higher goal. The class discussions stimulated points of view that differed from one's own, and often the discourse was at a college level. One learned to listen, think about what was said, and tried to formulate an appropriate response My classes were riveting in more ways than one.

Geometry, a second-year requirement in the math sequence, was taught by the young and alluring Miss Eleanora Gelsinger. The knit dress she wore daily clung to the contours of her lithe body, and every male eye in the class assiduously followed the curves and angles of her geometry. The female students in her class liked and regarded her as one of their own. At the faculty–student volleyball game, her female students cheered her scores lustily. She brought a lively appreciation of math to the school. Math honors classes were fully subscribed when Eleanora was the faculty advisor but did not decline when the elderly Mrs. Freida Straus took over. "Aitchpe" (HP) students were serious. The year of geometry was delightful, but I had another interest after school.

Robert Frazin and I developed a fascination for radio broadcasting. Television was just capturing public appeal, but in the early 1950s radio was still the medium of choice for news, sports, and entertainment. Bob and I met after school at his home at 6932 South Jeffrey Avenue in affluent South Shore. Bob had a broadcast studio set up in the family dining room that had a radius range of two or three city blocks. Our audience was Sidney Pollock and one or two other classmates whom we enjoined to listen to our broadcasts of news, popular music, and drama scripts that we wrote. Our studio broadcast stories of war, adventure, and derring-do set me on a path of writing. In college, I hosted a classical music radio program.

Another positive influence in high school was Csaba Zoltani, an immigrant lad from Hungary. As the Soviets approached Budapest during the Second World War, Csaba's family fled with the Nazis to Germany and from there to the United States. A top student, Csaba was vehemently anti-Soviet and looked to the day when the communists would be driven from his homeland. Our interests were playing chess and learning about our cultural backgrounds. We visited each other's homes, dined together, and attended church services together. Csaba found it unseemly that I kissed my priest's hand in receiving antidoron (a piece of bread given after church service), something Presbyterians would not do.

During my junior year, I took lunch with a motley crew of miscreants. We were clandestine smokers and took to the park across from the school to do the dirty weed. One was Gene Tippet, who rejected his father's family name of Lillstrom and took his mother's maiden name. His sister, Kay Carol Lillstrom, told me of the bitter breakup between their parents and how it wounded both her and her brother when they were young. At the time, in the '50s, divorce was rare, and as for someone whose parents were joined at the hip, I found the idea of parents divorcing strange and disturbing. Gene's art filled the school gallery.

Luke Daniluc was a James Dean-like character whose shiny black 1949 two-door Oldsmobile Rocket carried us to football games. Years later in the film *Rebel Without a Cause*, actor James Dean fully captured the persona of Luke. After the game, cheerleaders would pile in his car, as many as could, to celebrate the win or loss of the day. Like a few young men who hung out at Hyde Park, Luke was cool, exciting to be with, but not a student. He dropped out of school and took a job at the steel works in South Chicago. His car would pull up to the school late afternoons to see classmates, but he showed up less and less as the barriers of education and social class emerged.

Sally Rooney, a tough Irish girl, was a good poet with a cynical and bitter view of life. Mary Healy avidly supported racial integration of the private school clubs and was seen as an outsider by the so-called popular kids. Ellie Frieberg, a popular Tri Hi society member and a cheerleader, did not belong in the group philosophically; she just liked to smoke. She and Mary disagreed on issues but were close friends. Harold Shade was anything but a token Black member of the group. He was at the center of our activities and discussions. Interracial dating was an accepted practice in our group but eschewed by the larger Hyde Park community. Politically the members of our group were left of center, but I was viewed as a reactionary. Hondo, a Chicago policeman, patrolled the environs for smokers and drug addicts, and was to be avoided.

In high school, I was not a model student, as evidenced by three suspensions: two for fist fights and one for smoking in the park across from the school. Hondo, the eagle-eyed cop, spied the canopy of cigarette smoke over a bush and turned me in as the lit cigarette burned a hole in my jacket pocket. The fist fight with Bruce Pertle began as an incursion into my personal property. The fight started at the stairwell, went down the stairs, and we broke into a home room between class periods. Bruce pushed me, I fell on my back, and his knee was on my chest with an outstretched fist ready to pounce, when a burly senior football player grabbed his arm, pulled us both up by the neck, and threw us out of the classroom. Unfortunately, word got out about the incident, and we were suspended for two days. Bruce and I remained friends, and he respected my space and property from then on. The other expulsion was over an incident in the lunchroom, where I threw a classmate on a table of food for calling me a smart-ass Greek. We Greeks have a way with food. My father and I were called to Assistant Principal Edward Small's office, where he read the riot act to me. Surprisingly, dad took my suspensions without reproach but assigned some extra dirty jobs for me at the store. As a seventeen-year-old, dad, too, had his share of fights while working at his uncles' candy store.

In 1908, as a newly landed immigrant, my dad, Peter, worked at the Noble Street candy store that belonged to his uncles Gus and Joseph. Behind the counter of the near west side shop were baseball bats ready for troublemakers, often drunk and usually belligerent, who would enter the store for a handout or to haze the staff. They created this discord simply because the owners were Greek immigrants who spoke English with an accent. Greek-owned luncheonettes, bars, ice cream parlors, and grocery stores often suffered such travail. Ironically, as is often the case with ethnic prejudice, the ruffians' parents or grandparents were immigrants themselves. Perhaps resentment was the basis for such animosity toward newcomers who had established a business and prospered. However, when the trouble got out of hand, the bats would come out, the miscreants were threatened with force, at times ending with a scuffle and minor bruises, until peace was restored. Occasionally, trouble at the store turned deadly.

My 60-year-old Uncle Gus (my grandfather's brother) also owned a cleaning shop at 855 North Ashland Avenue in Chicago when Leo Proch, along with two other intoxicated men, tried to enter the shop after hours to get their hands on the undeposited weekly cash. After shattering the plate glass front window, Leo tried to enter the premises. Gus threatened him with a gun, but Proch continued his efforts get in. As Proch crawled through the broken glass, Gus fired, struck Proch in the head, and killed him. Proch's companions fled. According to the news account in the June 24, 1934 issue of the *Chicago Tribune,* the 32-year-old Proch was married, a father, and lived at 918 North Ashland Avenue. Proch lived a block away from the store and was my uncle's neighbor yet had so little regard for the Greek immigrant shop owner that robbing him was an option. No doubt alcohol played a role in this incident, but tragically it was repeated many times as immigrant Greeks were forced to protect life and limb and, unfortunately, sometimes were themselves killed.

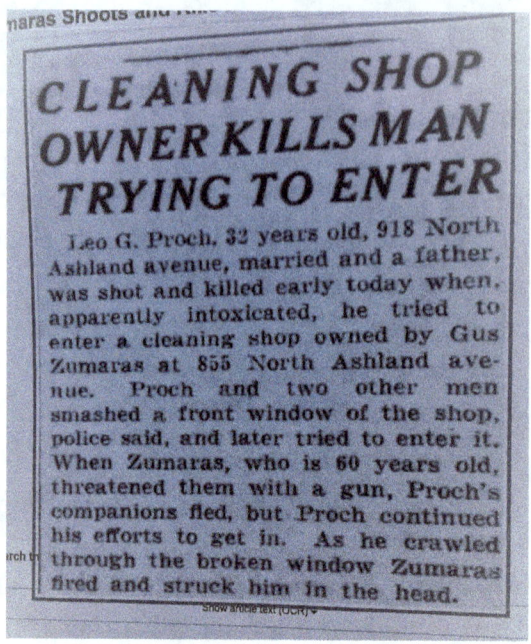

CHICAGO TRIBUNE, JUNE 24,1934

It was such intrusions into Greek businesses that led to the establishment of the America Hellenic Educational Philanthropic Association (AHEPA) in 1922 to fight discrimination, bigotry, and hatred felt by American citizens of Greek descent at the hands of nativists and the Ku Klux Klan. AHEPA promotes education of Greek Heritage and underwrites many philanthropic and charitable projects for the modern-day victims of *omogenia* (diaspora) in both Greek and American society. Such was the era of bank robbers, gangsters, and the law-abiding citizens who were suffering in the depression.

During senior year, in Dr. Sloan's American literature class, I polished my appreciation of stories and found narrative a preferred way of learning. We read many fine novels, including Ernest Hemingway's *For Whom the Bell Tolls,* and F. Scott Fitzgerald's *The Great Gatsby.*

The stories revealed the Aristotelean idea that tragedy imitates the actions of the best or noblest people of a society, that their action is consequential, and that their fall is great. We read the poems in Walt Whitman's *Leaves of Grass,* which highlighted his individuality, love of nature, and sexuality. For a class assignment, I wrote a short story about Whitman's love affair with Fannie Ferns that yielded a beautiful lawn, which was symbolic of the tapestry of the American people. This mockery and mixed metaphor cracked up the class and Dr. Sloan, who said that I had potential to make something of myself. In this high-level academic school, I graduated roughly in the middle of the class, but it was enough for entry to college.

My education extended beyond the walls of Hyde Park. My brother, David, received a scholarship for art classes at the school of the Art Institute of Chicago at 111 South Michigan Avenue, next to Grant Park. I was required to accompany David to his class, wait in the art museum, and bring him home safely in the afternoon. We clambered aboard the Illinois Central train at the south 74th street station on Saturday mornings and rode south through the Hyde Park and Kenwood districts, past Chinatown, and into the terminal at Randolph Street and Michigan Avenue. Along the way, we saw large housing projects under construction to the west and Burnham Park to the east that extended along the Lake Michigan coast to Grant Park. As we exited, we passed the floral stand of our uncles Tom and Gus Metos and their assistant, Ernie, who eventually bought the business when they retired. We stopped and chatted with the uncles and proceeded south on Michigan Avenue to the school.

During the two hours that I waited for David, I wandered through the exhibits of the Art Institute, which was like passing through a chronicle of world creativity. The exhibits were organized in historical periods, beginning with the ancient world of Greece and Rome and the early medieval period of relics, armor, and religious icons. Then one entered the Renaissance period of European art, in which there was a marked change from biblical themes to the real-life secular content of portraits, still life, and nature. This was followed by the modern period of impressionist and post-impressionist art. I would spend time in the gallery, thinking about the images of the smartly dressed man and woman in Gustave Caillebotte's *Paris on a Rainy Day* and the architecture that city planner Georges-Eugene Hausmann had revitalized in the Parisian neighborhood, which formed the background of the painting. The great impressionist Georges Seurat used points of color to represent the rich and poor elements of Parisian society in his *A Sunday Afternoon on the Island of the Grande Jatte.* I looked at the figures in these paintings, wondered about who they were, their lives, and how they were like or different than people I knew. The experience of viewing these works of art from different periods was profound. I saw that modern art and modern science were on parallel tracks toward the end of the 19th century. In my chemistry class, I learned that Russian chemist Dmitri Mendeleev broke down physical matter to create the periodic table of the elements. About the same time, Georges Seurat broke down color pigments to create works of art. Both school learning and learning on one's own leads to a well-formed education.

The end of senior year was festive as I joined classmates to party. My parents had purchased a new blazing red two-tone 1955 Mercury sedan. Since my parents did not drive, I was charged with driving duties and used the car to travel to school on occasion, and my popularity rose. Classmates Melba Maltenfort and Jane Kontos gave large parties the week before graduation that were open to all seniors, but the former attracted Jewish students and Jane's party mostly Christians. I attended both, but Jane's party was self-revelatory.

The Kontoses were a large, well-to-do Greek family who lived in a four-story gated mansion at 4624 South Ellis Avenue, Chicago. At the party, I peeked into the cavernous kitchen as Jane's four adult brothers and father sat at a large table eating their late dinner soup, with a rack of lamb, hot off the grill, cooling on the counter, and large chunks of broken bread on the table; I found the masculine and almost medieval scene arresting. Jane and I attended the St. Constantine and Helen Church at 7351 South Stony Island Avenue and were Greek Orthodox Youth Association (GOYA) members. Jane was a fine Greek American girl, much like the girl that my mother and father felt that their sons should marry. She was family oriented, pulled her weight in the family business, was deeply religious, and would make a perfect mother and respectful daughter-in-law. There was no ambiguity about my parents' wishes in the choice of a mate for me. My wife was to be Greek American and from a good family. Jane fit their qualifications perfectly. I believe that this parental demand was the crux of the conflict I felt between the embrace of my Greek identity and the desire to push away my Greekness.

For the children of immigrants, adaptation to both the family's original culture, be it Greek or Dominican, and the majority culture, be it American or Canadian, is essential. If the adaptation is assimilation, the original culture is rejected, and the majority culture is adopted. For instance, the children do not learn the language (e.g., Greek), do not participate in its religious and cultural activities, and instead fully adopt the norms, practices, and values of the majority culture. When it comes to the choice of a marriage partner, the mate typically comes from the majority culture, and family support declines. Two of my wife's brothers, Steve, and Nick, assimilated; they had a scant knowledge of Greek, saw themselves as Americans, and married non-Greeks.

On the other hand, if the adaptation is integration, the original culture and language are embraced, and majority culture values and morals are adopted. Depending on the choice of a marriage partner, family support may be conflicted. If the partner is Greek, then there is family support for the marriage. If the partner is not Greek and the family desires a Greek partner, then the family and the child may be in conflict. This is a situation in which the immigrants have maintained their identity, but the child has integrated. Obviously, cultural stress is present in both assimilation and integration but is greater in the former without family social support; stress also can be great on children, who are often torn between assimilation and integration, between preserving family ties or fraying them.

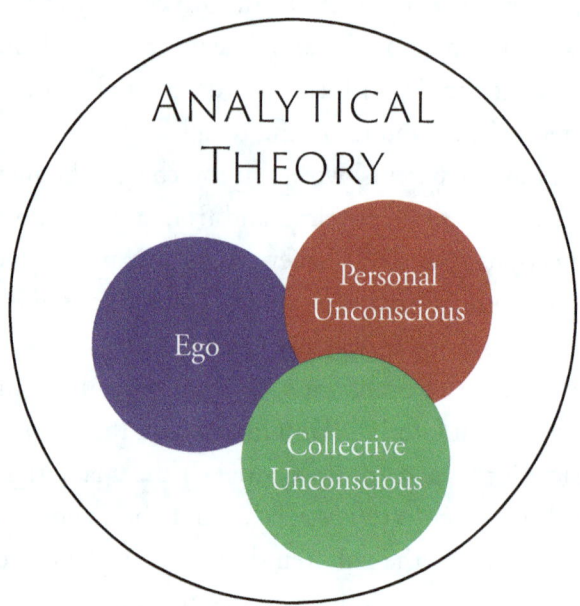

Adolescence is the beginning of individuation, an integral part of psychologist Carl Jung's Analytical Theory. It involves the process of coalescing the conscious and unconscious mind, such that the person becomes a distinct personality from all others. The self or ego becomes unified with the personal unconscious and what Jung calls the collective unconscious—that aspect of the unconscious that all humans share. The mother–child bond is an example of the collective unconscious present in all human cultures. When a bond is missing between mother and child, the child fails to individuate fully. The bond between son and father is also part of the collective unconscious and significant to gender and role identity. The self or ego is the center of the field of consciousness, which contains our conscious awareness of existing and a continuing sense of personal identity. The world we experience, our awareness of others, and our self-awareness are expressed through the ego. Self-esteem is damaged when the individual feels guilt or shame. As a result, individuation is impeded. At the personal unconscious level, our conflicts find contention, but we are often unaware of what is brewing deeper in the unconscious.

Jane Kontos and I were classmates, belonged to the same church and youth groups, and lived in the same neighborhood. Although our family finances differed, both families were broadly in the same social class. Moreover, Jane was a nice young girl. From my mom's perspective, someone like Jane, who is Greek, would be the ideal person for me to invite to the prom. No doubt that my dad would concur. If I invited Jane to the prom, I would be in harmony with my parents' wishes. On the other hand, if I invited another person—

YEARBOOK PORTRAIT, GEORGE, JUNE 1955

say, a Kay Carol Lillstrom, who is Swedish and from a dysfunctional family—this would pose concern for my parents. Why, when there is a lovely Greek girl nearby, would I venture to invite someone outside of our group, a *xenie?* The girl may be a fine person, but she does not share our language, religion, or values of Greekness. To my parents, going with a Kay would not make sense when a Jane was available. This dilemma of an integrating immigrant youth with his very Greek parents occurred at the conscious level and the unconscious level, creating conflict at both levels. In a sense, the bond between parents and son was challenged and formed unconscious discord. Thus, my personal unconscious and collective unconscious were in disharmony, and individuation was impeded.

My parents were not aware that Jane Kontos was perhaps available to invite to the prom; nor were they in any sense aware of Kay Carol Lillstrom or even of my intention to ask someone to the senior prom. It was an unconscious conflict. Though I was aware of my parents' strong feelings and attitudes, I told myself that they would not care that I took a non-Greek girl to the prom. On the other hand, I also knew that in protest of my first cousin Susan's wedding to a non-Greek my father did not attend the ceremony. I both believed and did not believe in my parents' disfavor toward the choice. Herein lies the conflict: I was of two minds, and as a result, I believe impeded the integrity of my personal development for the next decade of my life.

I pulled the bright red Mercury in front of Kay Carol's house. Corsage in hand, I went to the door and in my politest manner greeted Mrs. Lillstrom, gave assurances that her daughter would be as safe as a virgin princess carrying a cup of gold on the silk road from Beijing to Samarkand, arriving home with her gold and virginity intact. And off we went to the senior prom at the Palmer House Hotel.

SEVEN

GO WITH
THE FAT CATS

The mind is not a vessel that needs filling,
but wood that needs igniting.
—Plutarch

Telemachus imitates his Mentor's pronunciations
and his drinks. . . and gastronomy.
—Herzen

The question of whether the impact of injury to an infant's brain is greater or lesser than a like injury to an adult's brain was one I had not pondered until Professor Donald Scharlock invited me to join his research team at the psychology laboratory at Roosevelt University. After the last session of the learning theories class that he taught, he and I were walking back to his office when he asked what I planned to do after completing my undergraduate studies the following year. Without much certainty, I mumbled something about touring Europe. "Well come to the lab; you may find some things more interesting than Europe." This suggestion by the man who was to become my mentor and friend set me on a course of a lifetime study of mind and brain and becoming a university professor in psychology. But every life unfolds in context—and at that time I was still an undergraduate, an undistinguished one at that, taking college classes during a unique period in America.

The 1950s through the very early 1960s was a period of prosperity in the United States. Dwight Eisenhower was president, and the American economic engine was throwing off automobiles, superhighways, fossil fuel energy, planes, trains, appliances, and electronic products in vast quantity. In the process, the country grew richer. Interest rates were low and stable; the equities market had shaken off years of slumber, and the value of "nifty fifty" Dow stocks wase growing; employment was high, and U.S. products were the envy of the world. The economy overall grew by 37% during the 1950s, and unemployment remained low, about 4.5%. At the end of the decade, the median American family had 30% more purchasing power than at the beginning. Inflation was minimal, in part because of Eisenhower›s efforts to balance the federal budget.

The social matrix was healthy. Family life was paramount and protected. Men and women married young, and grew with their several children, adding to the burgeoning population. Grandparents at age 50 were common, and men gave up work in their 60s, securing their retirement with Social Security, a pension, and their life savings. Restrictive laws made it difficult to obtain a divorce; a long separation period and financial settlement favored the wife and children. Consequently, divorce was rare, more or less limited to celebrities and those able to afford a trip to Nevada for a quickie divorce. Abortion and homosexuality were uncommon, or so we thought.

The politics of the fruited plain were moderate, slightly to the right of center, and the bilateral foreign policy drew support from both parties in concord. Paradoxically, the Democrats pushed for larger military funding, while, predictably, the Republicans pushed for fiscal restraint. Attitudes were firmly anti-communist, and the

Soviet Union was seen as a threat to world peace, thereby requiring a strong and well-financed military. Church attendance was high. During the 1950s, nationwide church membership grew at a faster rate than the population, jumping from 57 percent of the U.S. population in 1950 to 63.3 percent in 1960. Americans were joiners of clubs—book clubs, women's clubs, men's clubs, bowling leagues, knitting circles, sports clubs, dance clubs. More than 150,000 social, recreational, and sports clubs met on a regular basis throughout the decade, providing a medium for social cohesion outside of the home. Differences among the social classes were muted, and a homogeneity in attitudes prevailed. The income disparity between the well off and the poor was narrow. For instance, in the 1950s, a typical CEO merely made 20 times the salary of the average worker, whose salary was about $3500. Americans ate the same breakfast, dressed much the same way, and vacationed in the United States rather than abroad. Most Americans completed high school and 5% attended college, limited largely to bright students. An ethic of hard work, achievement, independence, community service, and saving for the future prevailed. But the period had a dark side of social practices that reached back centuries.

Prejudice and discrimination were rampant toward non-white races. Blacks, Hispanics, and Asian citizens were victims of bias in employment, housing, education, and services. In the southern states, Jim Crow laws were designed to prevent minorities, and at times majorities, from voting. Prejudice also extended to Jews, Catholics, and southern Mediterranean races, though to lesser degree. The thrust of such unfairness was mainly to prevent interracial marriage and social relationships between whites and other races. In fact, there were laws that forbade interracial marriage in the southern states, and red lining restricted housing to blacks in both the South and North.

However, the 1950s was also a period in which some of these restrictions were removed. The brutal murder of Emmitt Till and the failure of the State of Mississippi to convict the murderers precipitated an outcry that bolstered civil rights movements. Protests and civil action brought about the opening of education to blacks when President Eisenhower forced Arkansas to allow interracial school attendance. It was not until 1964 that Congress passed Public Law 88-352 (78 Stat. 241), which was signed by President Lyndon Johnson. The Civil Rights Act of 1964 prohibits discrimination on the basis of race, color, religion, sex or national origin. Discrimination was stripped from the public square but remained in varying degree in the minds and hearts of many Americans. Nonetheless. black and white Americans in college strove to achieve their life goals in tolerance of one another. I was one such college student in 1955.

Perhaps the idea of academic work lay buried in the back of my mind and possibly in my temperament. As an adolescent, I preferred listening to my collection of Bach's Brandenburg concertos and Mozart's operas—Cosi Fan Tutti a favorite. As for reading, Ayn Rand's *The Fountainhead* and *Atlas Shrugged* fed my propensity toward life-long conservatism and perhaps selfishness. Despite growing up in the church and doing a stint as an altar boy, by the time I was 15, I questioned the authority of the church in personal behavior and the nature of the world. A growing interest in science, particularly biology, replaced Christ's teachings, but nevertheless I retained the idea of an omnipresent God as the creator of the universe. I approached our young, charismatic priest, Fr. Basil Gregory, about Darwin's theory of evolution after a youth meeting. Distracted as he was in wrapping up the meeting, he said, "That's a question we need to take up at another time." We never did. I judged that the church had no answer to evolution theory. Nor did I reach out to the priest to follow up on my query, perhaps to preserve the idea that science had answers and the church did not. Yet God remained a presence, and the idea of reconciling the spiritual with the material continued to occupy my thoughts and concerns.

Throughout my high school and college years, work in the family store took up much of my time. So, when the opportunity for me to

GEORGE IN HIS SODA JERK DAYS

join the psychology department laboratory came up, it cut into the time that I would be available to work at the store, leaving the others to carry the load in my absence. As I was completing my undergraduate work and spending time in graduate study, less and less time was devoted to the store, until I finally left altogether. It was a burden on my family but necessary to complete my education.

The Psychology Laboratory at Roosevelt University was a unique facility for conducting research with humans and animals. It also served as a teaching lab for the physiological psychology course, where sheep brain specimens were dissected as the practical class activity to learn brain structure and function. The research lab included a vivarium that housed laboratory rats and cats. Initially, my function was to see that the animals were fed and their waste removed. There was also a soundproof auditory test chamber for experiments on hearing, a surgical operating room, an electronics workshop, and an office for the senior lab assistants.

The lab's director, Donald Scharlock, had completed a post-doctoral grant at the University of Chicago on the neuroscience of audition when he returned to Roosevelt University as full professor of psychology and chairman of the psychology department. With several U.S. government and private grants, he established the psychology laboratory and revised the curriculum to include courses on the biology of behavior, all at the age of 34 years. Born in Erie County, New York of German immigrant parents, he maintained a proletariat "them and us" outlook on life. After a stint in the army at the end of WWII, he earned bachelor and doctoral degrees at the University of Buffalo under the mentorship of distinguished Professor B. R. Bugelski. Professor Scharlock was married to Nidia Thomas, a clinical psychologist; they had five children and lived in a brownstone in the Hyde Park section of Chicago. A dynamic and forceful lecturer, he attracted many students and added highly qualified instructors to the psychology program. Experimental psychologists like Scharlock placed their faith in data derived from controlled research on the relationship between brain and behavior. In a sense, in 1960 psychology was on the cusp of an era in which the field of neuroscience would be launched and integrated with psychology, neuroanatomy, psychiatry, and physiology. Such study requires scientists to be trained in several disciplines: biology, chemistry, physics, and psychology. Scharlock foresaw these changes and impressed them on us, his charges at Roosevelt.

Donald Oldling Hebb, perhaps the most influential psychologist of the 20th century, transformed thinking about how the brain relates to conscious experience. In his 1949 book, *Organization of Behavior*, Hebb argued that every experience a person encounters

PROFESSOR DONALD SCHARLOCK

becomes set into the network of brain cells. Then, each time a certain action or thought is repeated, the connection between neurons is strengthened, changing the brain, and strengthening the learning. A constructionist, Hebb argued that plasticity of neural connections allows the brain to adapt to an injury, such as stroke, by forming new connections. Based on the theory, Hebb predicted that brain injury suffered in infancy was less debilitating in adulthood, than trauma suffered in adulthood. It was this hypothesis that Scharlock's research team sought to test—specifically, that brain injury in infant kittens, tested as adult cats, would show fewer deficits in hearing than brain injuries in adult cats.

Our laboratory was staffed by two senior lab assistants, Avram (Sonny) Yarmat and Thomas Tucker, who were engaged in research projects with Dr. Scharlock that they hoped to publish and present along with their applications to doctoral programs. The other lab assistants—Sam DeNosquo, Michael Miller, and I—were the junior members of the team and given the less demanding jobs (making sure the lab was clean, seeing that the surgery instruments were sterilized).

Nonetheless, we observed and learned lab protocol and took in the intricacies of conducting a research project.

The work of our laboratory concerned the function of the cortex (the outer layer of the brain) devoted to hearing in cats. In today's terms, the work was primitive. The basic design was to make selective lesions on both sides of the cat's auditory cortex and test whether the cat would learn to discriminate between sounds that were loud or softer, high or lower in pitch, or among different patterns of sounds. Typically, the ability to discriminate was tested when the cat avoided electric shock by choosing the correct signal. After massive lesions of the auditory cortex, adult-operated animals could learn to make discriminations of loudness and pitch but not of pattern of sounds like high–high–low versus, low–high–low.

The results of a published study by Scharlock and Yarmat (1962)[1] showed that auditory pattern discriminations cannot be acquired by the cat after a large bilateral (both sides of the brain) ablation of the auditory cortex at maturity. However, if such ablations are sustained during infancy, these discriminations are readily learned when the cat matures. The function of the cortex in auditory discrimination depends on the age of the nervous system at the time of injury. The research verified D.O. Hebb's theory on the effects of early and later in life brain damage.

We junior assistants were chomping at the bit to do research guided by Dr. Scharlock. However, the testing room and surgery were taken up by the seniors. Then good fortune struck: A position opened for a research assistant in neurology and psychiatry at Northwestern University's medical school, and Scharlock, having taken pity on my research doldrums, nominated me for the post. I was to test the touch discrimination of infancy-damaged macaques that were separated at birth from their mothers—another research project testing Hebb's theory on infant brain damage. After I applied and was accepted, Scharlock, in his blue-collar stance, said, "Go with the fat cats, George." This comment set me on a life course that I was to follow. I was to continue to work toward my MA degree at Roosevelt and retain my workload at its psychology lab, do research at Northwestern, and work at my parents' store. The last item, helping my parents, unfortunately got short shrift, but I managed to put in time at the store.

When I gingerly mentioned to my parents that I wanted to continue my study of psychology, they were understandably confused. For them a profession was medicine or law or, if one could not cut it, pharmacy. In fact, pharmacy may even have been the best choice in their reasoning; with a pharmacy license, the store could expand operations. These imaginings were stopped at my insistence on research psychology. My parents were mollified, that with two part-time jobs I was self-sufficient financially. In fact, my parents never supported me from the time I began work at the psychology and neurology lab at Northwestern's Feinberg School of Medicine.

The medical school housed a colony of macaque monkeys for research purposes. I was to observe and measure the behavioral adaptations of macaques as adults after parietal lobe (which mediates

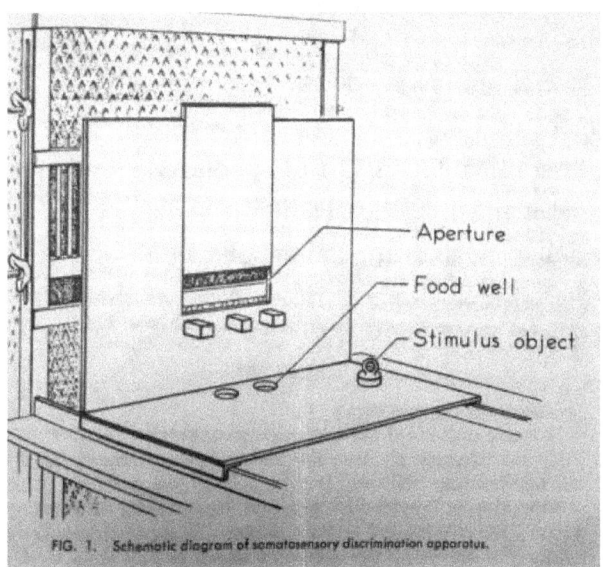

FIG. 1. Schematic diagram of somatosensory discrimination apparatus.

TACTILE DISCRIMINATION APPARATUS

touch) excision as infants. The purpose of the study was to determine whether parietal lobe damage in infancy was a possible factor in autism in children. Dr. Harry Harlow's classic research with infant macaques revealed that touch and contact comfort were crucial to bonding with the mother. It was suggested by other researchers that parietal lobe deficits or dysfunction in infants may be a factor in autism. The study also provided confirmation of D. O. Hebb's prediction of good sensory function in adults following early brain damage.

My role was to assist neurosurgeon resident Dr. Edir Sequeira to bilaterally resect the parietal lobes of five-day-old macaques and to see that they recovered from the surgery. The infants were then taken to home care by another assistant and allowed an average of 20 weeks for full recovery under filmed observation. The parietal lobe organizes touch, pain, and kinesthetic sensory experience. The sensation experienced in picking up a cup or grasping a doorknob are mediated by the parietal lobe in concert with other brain areas.

The mature animals were returned to the laboratory colony at Northwestern for testing of the tactile senses at age five months. The test apparatus, shown in the figure, permitted the animal to reach through the aperture and feel a stimulus object to match one of a choice of several objects. A food reward, typically fruit, followed a correct response.

In the discrimination tests that I conducted, the operated-on animals showed marked deficits. Preliminary training for the prompt and successful tactual manipulation of stimuli and rewards took 3 days in the normal animals, and 30 days for the operates, which showed impaired motor dexterity. On tasks combining vision and tactile cues, no differences were observed between normal macaques and operates. The operates failed to discriminate shapes* (triangle vs. square) and hardness (soft vs. hard); operates took 50% longer to master the discrimination of hardness. These results were reported in Volume IV of *Recent Advances in Biological Psychiatry* (1964).[2] What to make of the findings of the research?

Findings that show no difference between groups do not necessarily mean that a difference does not exist. Sample size and confounding factors may diminish an otherwise robust effect. A significant difference based on statistics may in reality be a sampling error rather than a true effect of difference between groups. With these caveats in mind, the study revealed differences and no differences between the operates and unoperated animals. The findings on tactile discrimination and grooming revealed impairment in the parietal operates. Social and play behavior revealed that operates engaged in normal primate behavior with other animals and their human caretakers. Thus, the hypothesis of parietal deficit as a source of autistic behavior was not supported. Furthermore, while D.O. Hebb's suggestion that infant brain injury is less debilitating than brain injury sustained by adults was not supported in this study, it showed that infant brain injury created severe deficits in operated animals.

To my classmates at the university, I was the dorky professor in the making. Judy Mendelsohn, a psychology major, was having difficulty understanding the concepts and experiments in learning theory class and was scoring low grades on quizzes. We had been in high school together, separated by a year. "Would you come over to my house tonight to go over some of this stuff," she implored. Judy was sophisticated and Jewish and had broken up with her boyfriend Mike Phillips, a cool Jewish guy, and a great athlete. When Judy opened the door to her home in the affluent South Shore area, I entered a milieu wholly astounding to my eyes. World-class art filled the walls, a sculpture stood in the reception hall, and the apartment contained room after room. Her father, Hyman Mendelsohn, was a lawyer specializing in trusts, as well as a banker. Judy's older brother Eric was writing his PhD thesis in analytical chemistry. So, the family was not only rich but smart, and, with some tutoring, Judy was doing well in class.

Judy and I dated for about six months, and she seemed blissfully unconcerned about the large discrepancy in our families' assets and lifestyles. In fact, she would visit our apartment over the store and appeared perfectly comfortable in relating to my family, particularly my brother, David. The situation at her home was different. When I would arrive for the tutoring, Judy's mother treated me as an alien presence; but then, the goy was okay, as long as he was helping, and not screwing her daughter. Judy had the ability to evoke an image that persisted in memory. For instance, she described the new Edsel's puckered grille as an Oldsmobile (with an oval grille) that swallowed a lemon. Things were going well with us, the tutoring long past, and I wondered if the tutoring had been merely a ploy to get to know me. Then I was shot down. As we were entering Judy's home, her mother's voice called from the recesses of the apartment, "Judy, Mike called." Judy ran down the hall, never to be seen again. I was the devastated dork.

After Judy vanished from my life, Scharlock informed me about what I and other senior-year psych students at Roosevelt were already aware of: Professor Goldman, the statistics instructor, had a weekend drinking problem and could not make his Monday morning introductory psychology lecture. In a reversal of academic protocol, Scharlock asked me to teach the Monday topic-of-the-week sessions, and Goldman would do the discussion sections. I was struck that he had asked me to step in, and assiduously prepared a lecture on Pavlov's learning theory, Scharlock's specialty. Entering the class, I surveyed the assembled students, row by row, and in the last row, the very last seat, sat Dr. Scharlock, meerschaum pipe clenched in mouth. My heart fell to the floor. I struggled to recover and find my voice. Fortunately, the detailed preparation that I had made carried the day, and the lecture flowed out oratorically. Once he determined that I could do the job, Scharlock got up and, without comment, walked out. In relief, the class clapped.

The junior assistants, Sam DeNosquo, and Michael Miller, added to the lively atmosphere of the Roosevelt laboratory. Outside of the lab in the student union, along with a motley crew of Greeks and liberal arts students, we made up the student apathy league (SAL), devoted to curbing enthusiasm. In the lab, however, we assisted in brain dissections with students and conducted research with serious attention; there was a family atmosphere, with the senior assistants guiding the research program and Scharlock in orbit directing the laboratory. At times, professors and students, male and female, would gather at nearby pubs for hamburgers and drinks. A nub of sexuality pervaded these drinking sessions.

After all, Kinsey's interviews with males and females revealed that sexuality was in the air. Kinsey's inquiries into human sex life led him to establish an institute and to publish *Sexual Behavior in the Human Male* (1948) and *Sexual Behavior in the Human Female* (1953). Based on over18,000 personal interviews, these reports indicated a wide variation in sexual behavior, including homosexuality, sadomasochism, pedophilia, and sex with animals. The reports also indicated that 37% of males and 13% of females claimed to have engaged in same-sex behavior to the point of orgasm. However, fewer than 10% of males were committed exclusively to same-sex partners. Initially, Kinsey's account of males was acclaimed for the excellence of his reportage and statistical techniques, and for the candor in revealing sexuality as it was practiced. The report on females, however, was condemned, and sales of the book were low. Kinsey was criticized for violating certain ethical and research standards, and the validity of the findings was questioned. Investigative reporting revealed that fraud and illegal practices took place at the institute. As a result, Kinsey's authority as a sexologist was stained. Nonetheless, his reports had a wide impact on social mores and sexual practices. Kinsey died in 1956, and by the early 1960s cultural attitudes toward sex and marriage were changing.

Occasionally, Scharlock would overdrink, and one of us would drive him home in his car, The others would follow and take the

SAM DeNOSQUO, GEORGE, MICHAEL MILLER

assigned driver home after he dropped Scharlock off. One evening Scharlock and I were alone drinking. We were close—not buddies, but teacher and student; once when he and his family went on summer vacation, I had stayed in his home in the burglar-ridden Hyde Park neighborhood to watch the house. That evening as I was negotiating the traffic on the drive to his home, he moved over close to the driver's side. His head dropped on my shoulder, and his hand fell on my thigh. The hit was obvious, even to my virgin innocence. A gentle shove and a "Time to get you home, Doc" moved him to the other side of the car. I dropped him off and took the bus home, shaken, a mentor tarnished. A week later I met Tom Tucker, a straight arrow, outside of the lab, and he sensed my concern. "Don gets out of control when the liquor in his blood is high. Enough said." No mention of the incident was ever made.

Don Scharlock supported my application to SUNY at Buffalo's PhD program with his mentor, the eminent B. R. Bugelski, who later became department chairman. With some teaching experience, and publication of the Northwestern medical school research, I was a strong candidate for admission. Recalling our initial exchange about my career, his last words to me were, "Always stay with the fat cats, and when you complete the doctorate, take that trip to Europe."

REFERENCES

1. Scharlock, D. P., & Yarmat, A. J. (1962). Avoidance learning as a function of trials per training session in normal brain operated cats. *Journal of Comparative and Physiological Psychology, 55*(4), 455–457. https://doi.org/10.1037/h0049175
2. Aarons, L., Shulman, J. L., Masserman, J., & Zimmar, G.P., (1964). *Behavioral Adaptations After Bilateral Parietal Ablation in the Neonate Macaque,* In Joseph Wortis (Ed.), *Recent Advances in Biological Psychiatry* (Vol. IV, pp. 347–361).

EIGHT

TRAVELS WITH MY SISTER: GREEK INFLUENCE IN EUROPE

When they asked Socrates where he came from, he did not say "From Athens" but "From the World."
—Michel de Montaigne

Early June mid-1960s: Colleges and universities disgorged their students, with some rushing to airports to catch charter flights for a summer in Europe. The airports were crowded with duffle bags, back packs, Samsonite matched luggage sets, and the long-forgotten battered suitcase from the attic that Dad carried on his job search from city to city after the war. Most travelled with a friend or a couple of friends—girls with girls, boys with boys. Boy–girl travel would come later, once the pill to prevent pregnancy had more adherents. Most youth were casually dressed, wearing Levis or slacks with a shirt or top; but there were traditionalists in coats and tie and dresses or skirts topped with a sweater set.

There is no better person to travel through Europe with than my sister Peggy (Panayiota). A dedicated Europhile, Peggy had lived with our sophisticated Greek family, who spoke English, French, and Italian, and she had absorbed the ways and ethos of Europe. Peggy had shed her American mannerisms and attitudes without peeling off her love of America. When she was a teen, she lived in Europe for a year, and our dad, Peter, had resolved to make a tour of Greece with Peggy and return to the U.S. with her. On the day of the passage home, Peggy still had not packed her luggage, hoping upon hope for a last-minute reprieve, but it was not to come. She returned to Chicago, ruefully completed high school and a bachelor's degree in education. And after a year of teaching in Chicago schools, was now preparing to return to Greece to live.

We landed at Gatwick Airport outside of London and took a couple of rooms at a bed and breakfast and toured the venerable sites of the city. London was the likely destination to make a first exotic encounter with a foreign land, so the American Express kiosk was jammed with youthful travelers seeking the exchange of dollars for pounds. London was ablaze with youth culture. The Beatles' rock band was on an ascending trajectory worldwide, denims were flared, shirts floral, and skirts mini, well above the knee. Hard drugs had

1960S FELLOW TRAVELERS

not yet hit the youth scene, but marijuana traveled hidden in back packs. With little knowledge or care of who Lord Horatio Nelson was or what he accomplished, young people nonetheless crammed his square, at the feet of British lions surrounding his eminence. Our plan was to go to Goteborg, pick up a P122 Volvo two-door sedan, and travel through Europe to Greece. So, we boarded a ship to traverse the North Sea to our destination.

It was Midsomer, the old single-smoke stack ship was Swedish, and the summer solstice celebrations were underway throughout the longest day of the year and into the shortened night. Our fellow passengers were Swedish young people returning home, or English youth on their way to visit Sweden. Cool ocean breezes prevailed, and a good deal of drinking warmed body and soul. Peggy and I made friends with our fellow travelers, and we enjoyed being the only Americans on board.

The North Sea is treacherous any time of the year. On the afternoon of the second day, a fierce summer squall hit the ship, and waves covered the bow all the way up to the forecastle. Glasses and plates slid to the floor. One of our friends, somewhat inebriated, was swept by a wave across the bow deck to the ship's rail but was able to get up and stagger to safety. The rest of the trip was uneventful, and

PEGGY WITH FRIENDS

we arrived in Goteborg harbor, rested and eager to go to the Volvo factory to pick up the car.

Cars in Sweden have steering on the left, but the opposing driving lane is to the right. So, traffic comes at you from the right and turning right involves crossing the opposite lane. Moreover, European cars are stick shift, involving a clutch pedal to shift gears, which can be tricky when on a slight incline, with cars behind you honking as you slide backward. Such were our travails as we left the Volvo factory and streamed into Göteborg traffic. Somehow, we made it to Malmö for the ferry to Copenhagen and the security of the right lane driving through our remaining travels.

Our plan was to take three weeks to visit major European cities that would include Hamburg, Brussels, Amsterdam, Paris, Geneva, Florence, Rome and push on to Brindisi for the crossing to Greece. That would give us a couple of days for each city and a day for driving in between. It would allow me about a month in Greece before my return home to the U.S. Peggy would stay in Greece.

In the course of our travels, we noted a distinct difference at that time in the cultures of the cities of northern and southern Europe. Our visit to Hamburg, a German port city, illustrates the apparent difference between North and South. Pedestrians on Hamburg street corners took care to obey crossing signals; in Italy last minute dashes across the street took place. A young woman walking alone in Malmö or Copenhagen could stride in security, her serenity undisturbed; in Milan or Athens she would receive unwanted attention and perhaps catcalls from males loitering in the streets. Bus schedule arrivals and departure times were strictly observed in Hamburg and Amsterdam, less so in Milan and Rome. An orderly reception at the hotel desk in Göteborg where we had made reservations was efficiently dispatched; in Paris after waiting for the desk clerk to arrive, we were greeted with a changed room arrangement. While the character of the cities differed, all charmed us.

In Hamburg we encountered a Greek. Peggy and I were speaking Greek, discussing which tour to take, when a voice called, "Eiste

PEGGY AND HECTOR, HAMBURG

Ellinas?" Our ανακριτής (interrogator) was a Greek seaman, Hector, from the island of Poros whose ship was unloading cut lumber at the dock. He shared his observations about life at sea and recommendations about places to visit in Hamburg.

We had just taken a photo of him and were chatting amiably, when he spied a man picking up a discarded ball point pen from the sidewalk. Hector ran to the man, tapped him on the shoulder and pointed to his shirt pocket. The man looked at Hector, looked at the pen, and gave him the pen. Hector came back to us and said, "The Germans are naive; they believe anything they are told. We Greeks are 'ponerie.'" [no direct translation; *poniros* means sly, discerning, clever, wicked—all of the above]. We saw that we were in the company of a slippery character and made a quick exit for a tour of the harbor. Our next stop was Amsterdam.

Another characteristic of Europeans was the dress code in those days of our travels. In Europe dress tended to be more formal than in the U.S. Of course, climate plays a role in how people dress, but nonetheless differences in formality prevailed. For men, jacket or suit, shirt with tie was common, even in recreational settings. Women dressed differently when out of the home. A dress, or skirt and top, makeup, and jewelry were the order of the day. Eveningwear tended to be even more formal. How one dressed said something about who you were, where you were from, and many took stock of appearance. On a streetcar, Europeans typically looked at other passengers' dress and accessories, and made a judgment of social class and status. One look at my shoes on a European street showed, "Ach, he is an American." In the U.S., dress between the social classes was considerably less distinctive and an indefinite predictor of social status. The billionaire H.L. Hunt dressed plainly, drove a low-end Chevrolet, and packed his own lunch. If you dressed like the rich, you might be rich but, then, you might not be. In the stories of Ring Lardner, and F. Scott Fitzgerald, dress could belie the character and status of the man. In the Music Man, the musical theatre creation of Meredith Wilson, a well-dressed flimflam man enters a town and tells the residents that he is something he is not, a musician.

Even the Greek philosopher Aristotle took care of his garments and appearance according to Timotheus, the Athenian (c. 446–357 BC):

PEGGY AND GEORGE, AMSTERDAM

Along with dressing well, he also wanted his hair to be fashionable and tidy. As for jewelry, according to Diogenes Laertius and his source, Aristotle enjoyed wearing rings and was conscientious of how he displayed them. From the quote, we also learned that Aristotle might have had a lisp, and his lifestyle was healthy enough to keep him fashionably slender. It is an incomplete picture, to be sure, but such details add a glimmer of humanity to the man who we otherwise know only through his written thoughts.[1]

It is perplexing to learn that the renowned Aristotle wore rings and cared about his appearance. However, as court tutor to Alexander, perhaps how one dressed mattered. A Spanish proverb holds that "Only God helps the badly dressed."

In Paris, we stood contemplating the statue of philosopher and bibliophile Michel de Montaigne (1533–1592). Our companion was Claudia, an American student studying at the Sorbonne. We contacted her through our dear friend, Gus Alevizos, a classmate of Claudia's in the U.S. The women appear somewhat uncertain as to why they are standing before Montaigne. But there is a good reason: He is an outstanding exemplar of the intellectual life of the West.

PEGGY AND CLAUDIA WITH MONTAIGNE, PARIS

If there was one person that Mortimer Adler, the editor of the University of Chicago's Great Books program, would appreciatively invite to dinner, it would be Montaigne, followed by Plutarch. Michel Montaigne's significance to our Western identity is that he channeled the great works of Greece and Rome to the Renaissance and to our times.

Montaigne's renowned library in his towered estate east of Bordeaux contained 1000 volumes of philosophy, history, poetry, and religion, arranged on five tiers of shelves in a semicircle.

It was here that Montaigne read Socrates' (the wisest man that ever was) steadfast address to the inpatient jurors of Athens in a Latin edition of Plato translated by Marsilo Fincino; here that he read Epicurus' vision of happiness in Diogenes Laertius *Lives* and Lucretius' *De Rerum Natura,* edited by Denys Lambin in 1563; and here that he read and reread Seneca in a new set of his works (strikingly suited to my humour) in a new set of his works printed in Basle.[2]

Montaigne, a polymath, authored over 30 books, most still in print, on almost every topic, and his influence is embedded in the curricula of every university. Peppered throughout his essays are references to and commentaries on the works of Greek and Roman writers. While erudite and learned, he made the distinction between book smarts and wisdom, and placed greater value on the latter. Wisdom involves the whole man or woman, including our sexuality, passions, and reflections. "True wisdom must involve an accommodation with our baser selves, it must adopt a modest view about the role that intelligence and high culture can play in any life and accept the urgent and at times deeply unedifying demands of our moral frame."[3]

When Michelangelo was asked how he created the beautiful 17-foot-high statue of the Biblical David, he said, "I merely chipped away the excess marble and the figure was revealed." And there it has stayed for centuries, right where it was created. The Galleria dell

'Academia was easily the high point of our visit to Florence. Unlike the equally beautiful, but damaged, marble statues of Greece—for instance, the Charioteer in the Museum of Delphi—all of the David's body parts were intact.

Often antiquarian statuary is damaged through the myriad of calamities that take place in its original setting. But more often when these items are stripped from the site of their origin, they are purposely or accidentally damaged. For instance, the Venus di Milo was found in pieces on the Aegean Island of Melos in 1820 and was subsequently presented to Louis the XVIII, who then donated it to the Louvre. Though the statue was reconstructed in a standing posture, the arms were never found.

The case sometime made by those who have removed antiquity from its original site is that it was an act of preservation and, that transplanted, the work was made available for viewing by the wider world. Nonetheless, once the antiquity's origin and ownership are determined, and the host government is willing and able to accept the item's return, it should be returned. Otherwise, the holder holds stolen goods.

VENUS DE MILO, PARIS

PATRAS HARBOR

As we entered Patras harbor, brilliant, white-painted homes of the city greeted us; the air was brisk, the waves sparkled with silver, and the sky was a Magritte blue. Confusion prevailed as we disembarked. Moving an automobile off a Greek ferry is a chaotic affair, with passengers. and vehicles nudging and pushing one another down the open gangway while other passengers and cars stand in a jumbled queue for a return trip to Brindisi. Adding to the din and bedlam on the docks were hawkers for guided tours, currency exchanges, taxis, and hotels. Such was our entry into Greece. It was an untidy scene, and I loved it. I was home.

Once in Athens, my sister and I were embraced by loving aunts, uncles, cousins, and various other family members. "Everywhere we went in Europe," we enthused, "we encountered the values of Greece."

REFERENCES

1. Hansley, C. K. The appearance of Aristotle. The Historian's Hut. https://thehistorianshut.com/2022/ 10/25/aristotle-59/
2. de Botton, A. (2001). *The consolations of philosophy* (pp. 116–17).
3. de Botton, A. (pp. 116–117)

NINE

BEAU FLEUVE

A River Runs Through it
—Norman Maclean.

A large bronze bison greeted me on my arrival at the Buffalo Central Terminal on Paderewski Drive, near Main Street and Memorial Drive. Plains bison did not roam the junction between the Great Lakes Basin and the Hudson–Mohawk River Valley, where the city was established, or so we thought. However, the idea that Buffalo was named Beau Fleuve (Beautiful River) by the French explorers when they first saw the Niagara River is an urban myth. Buffalo Creek first appears in print as part of the boundary description in the 1784 Treaty of Fort Stanwix between the fledgling United States and the Six Nation Confederacy. The New York State Museum's 1907 publication, *Aboriginal Place Names of New York*, cites extensive evidence of eastern woodland bison in this area, which makes a persuasive case for Buffalo Creek's name. I was admitted to the University of Buffalo graduate psychology program and fell in love with the area, especially the beautiful Niagara River flowing into the magnificent falls. In a sense, my entire life is like a beautiful river flowing from one experience to another, but at Buffalo it hit the falls.

On the road trip to Buffalo and return to Chicago a month before, my Dad and I got to know each other a little better. Research and college teaching were to be my life's work; the compensation was only sufficient, but the personal rewards were great. I think he understood my position. Thanks to a combination of assistantships, scholarships, and part-time work. my income as a student exceeded starting pay for college graduates, and in this my dad took pride. Pride of family and country is a Greek quality.

Years before, as a boy, I asked my dad which side I should choose to join if the United States and Greece were at war. He reflected for a moment and said that it would be a difficult decision to make for himself, but for me, "it should be easy; you are an American. We both share our Greek roots, and while I expect you to carry that distinctiveness forward, your loyalty is to your country. Your connection to Greece is merely ancestral. Your honor and duty is to the nation of your birth and my duty and honor is split, between Greece and the United States." However, the query revealed the deeper issue of our shared roots.

From my earliest boyhood, respect and pride of family were the first lessons learned about the Greek cultural trait of *philotimia*. No clear dictionary definition of philotimia exists. Rather, philotimo is a blend of qualities with honor, respect of parents, grandparents, and adult members of our family at the core, along with pride of country, ancestors, and generosity without expectation of return. For instance, my dad put off marrying for years, until he arranged his to bring his younger brother to the US and establish him in a business, broker his sister's marriage, and set up a home for the couple to live; he also supported his parents, Gioryios and Panayiota, in Greece until their finances were secure. A person with philotimo is aware that his behavior reflects on his family and does the right thing because his duty is to do the right thing. Sometime the lines between right and wrong are blurred, but we know in our hearts what is the right thing to do. Once I was in the corner of the back yard with a friend, when my dad came to the porch and twice called for me to come home. I pretended not to hear him, but he saw me, and he turned his back and went into the apartment. Dad did not say anything about my failure to respond. I burned with shame over my disrespect to his dignity, such that I could not look at my father, and I deeply regret that failing of philotimo, to this day.

In Buffalo, my dad and I had selected a place for me to live in the home of Mrs. Ruth Samuels, an elderly widow. A petite woman in her 70s, she had recently lost her husband and opened a rental bedroom and a room to study in her colonial home in Amherst, NY, a mile walk to Townsend Hall, which housed the psychology department. Ruth, an Orthodox Jew, offered a separate cabinet shelf for my plates and utensils and separate Tupperware for my food in the refrigerator. Ruth and I maintained separate space and schedules, except on September 15, 1961, when we watched the newly completed Berlin Wall on television, with East Germans attempting to escape. Sadly, she said it reminded her of the plight of Jews trying to escape from Germany in the 1930s.

On my arrival in Buffalo by train, someone had rifled my luggage in the baggage car. I discovered that two winter coats my mother had stuffed in the suitcase were missing, leaving me without outerwear for protection from the winter storms soon to arrive. I made repeated contact with the NY Central Railroad about recompense, to no avail. My classmate and friend Bonnie McDonald invited me to her family's home in the exclusive Williamsville suburb for dinner, where I mentioned my quest with the railroad. It turned out that Bonnie's dad was a NY Central executive and though he made no promise, I received a check about a week later.

Bonnie was what might be called a visual thinker. Her verbal skills were high, but she also excelled in math and statistical reasoning and was easily the top student in the psychology graduate program in these areas. Research divides visual thinkers into spatial and object visualizers. The former think in abstract patterns and the latter in photorealistic images. An object visualizer, Bonnie described how she would approach a math or statistics problem. She had a visual memory image of the digits from one to 100 as a spiral curling upward, and numbers beyond were seen as decagons—10-sided images—a small decagon for 100s and a large one for 1000s. For instance, 2,455 would be an image in the large decagon encircling the smaller at 2000 and 400, with 55 in the spiral. Visual thinking is not encouraged in traditional math classes in elementary and high school. Shop, music, art classes, and the chess team provide settings for developing these thinking skills but, regrettably, are often the first to be defunded in schools. Neuroscience and neuroanatomy, which involve imaging the brain, also comprises visual thinking, and this was helpful in my studies.

Bonnie and I stopped seeing each other at the end of our first year but remained friends through our time in graduate school.

A year later Lennie Jacobson, a classmate and I were passing through the Albright Knox Gallery, when a painting of Miss Rosamond Croker by the English portraitist Sir Thomas Lawrence stunned Lennie. "Wow, she looks like Bonnie McDonald. Fool, why did you leave her go?"

This was a good question that did not make sense in terms of the head, but for the heart it was another matter. Bonnie was a warm, intelligent, and thoughtful young woman who gave much to our relationship and would made a wonderful soulmate. However. much as I tried, somehow the sparks of a loving bond were missing. The things we shared were of the mind, but for some reason my feelings were left out of the picture. Bonnie married a classmate—a good, caring individual. I believe that their marriage was a happy one.

At the end of my first year, I had declared an interest in physiological psychology, later described as biopsychology and still later as a subdivision of neuroscience. Professor Jim (C.J.) Smith had just arrived from the University of Michigan to launch the biopsychology program at University of Buffalo (which that year became State University of New York at Buffalo, SUNY). C.J. Smith had a U.S. Public Health Service grant for his research, and a substantial grant from the university to build a biopsychology research laboratory. In those rich days of building universities, money was free-flowing and plentiful. The university that year appointed Nobel Laureate John Eccles as distinguished professor of neuroscience. As Dr. Smith's assistant, my task that summer was to set up the laboratory for him to carry on his research, and I found myself in a cutting-edge research field in psychology.

C.J. was born and schooled in the Buffalo area but completed his PhD at McGill University in Montreal under the mentorship of the eminent and influential neuroscientist D.O. Hebb. A dedicated bachelor, Smith spoke three languages, was a devotee of classical music, the outdoors, and railroads. We spent the summer painting the lab walls after C.J. spent a couple of days thinking about the color scheme. The electronic equipment came in, but days were spent contemplating placement. Over the summer there were no deliberations between us about the research. In the fall, I enrolled in neuroanatomy and neurophysiology courses at the UB medical school but resolved to do my dissertation with the department chair, B. R. Bugelski. I also made an alteration in my living arrangement that was life changing.

Ruth Samuels was sad to see me go, but I needed a place with privacy and freedom to do my cooking and socialize with classmates. Over the summer, I moved into the basement of a split-level home on Grange Road with a separate entrance and a pool. In contrast to my previous landlord, a professional couple, Robert, and Julia Newsome, and their young child, Karen, would collect my monthly rent. The apartment came with an undergraduate roommate, Daniel Rosenberg, a senior, who was planning to apply to a clinical psychology graduate program. We were a cozy household when Danny returned in September. Karen, age 6, would tumble downstairs to our apartment to play and once shared a momentous event with us.

In a television address on October 22, 1962, President John Kennedy notified the American public about the presence of missiles, explained his decision to enact a naval blockade around Cuba, and made it clear the U.S. was prepared to use military force if necessary to neutralize this perceived threat to national security. Following this news, we feared, along with the nation, that we were on the brink of nuclear disaster. Karen saw that Danny and I were concerned, and this disturbed her mood. We put on a happy face, sang her favorite songs, and calmed her with a glass of milk.

Growing up in the 1950s, my generation had the dread of nuclear war drilled into us with mock exercises, hiding in hallways or under our desks. Paradoxically, children of the '50s grew and developed with an optimistic outlook. Perhaps we stored our anxiety in the unconscious, However, it was not uncommon to know someone with a home bomb shelter provisioned with food and water, which was also a secret place to play. Somehow, we distanced ourselves from the threat of nuclear war. A few days after Kennedy's TV address, the Cuban crisis that unsettled the nation abated, and we resumed our activities. But as it did for Karen, the experience shattered our security.

Another thing that disturbed Karen was her parent's troubled marriage. Robert was a successful lawyer with a growing practice, so the family finances were in order. He and Julia had a comfortable home and an apparently loving relationship, but there were tensions in the marriage. Robert was bisexual, and when life's stresses or the marriage would hit a snag, he would take off for a sexual encounter with another man. Having lived with the family the year before I moved in, Danny was familiar with the situation in conversations he had with Julia. Both Robert and Julia were in therapy with a family counselor. When I returned to Buffalo from a weekend break, I was surprised to learn that Robert had moved out of the house and had taken up a relationship with a young woman in his office. Danny counseled Julia, but she was not distressed and accepted the breakup.

Like some women who were prevented from achieving their educational potential, Julia Lindner had a need to attain recognition of her intellectual gifts. A top student in high school, her parents, nonetheless, did not support a college education for their daughter. Instead, she was enrolled in Katherine Gibbs secretarial school for training in supporting business executives. Julia typed 80 words per minute, would correct the grammar and syntax of her boss's memoranda, and rewrite the company annual report, yet remained in low paying secretary. While living at New Haven, she met Robert Newsome, a law student, shared an apartment with him, until she became pregnant, and they married. Upon completion of his law degree, she and Robert, at her insistence, moved to the Buffalo suburb near the university. Robert quickly established a successful law practice and Julia became a stay-at-home mom, with her mental potential unfulfilled. Accordingly, she developed a circle of university friends and rented out the lower level of their home to graduate students. In many ways, a quest for intellectual attainment defined Julia and attracted her to those who had achieved some measure of academic success.

During the Thanksgiving break, Danny went home to Albany, and I remained in Buffalo to work on my course term papers. Julia would come down. with and without Karen, from time to time. We would talk and, frankly, I found her engaging, clever, and sexy.

At age 23, I was a virgin. Not that my relationships with women were sexless, but the sexual revolution had not hit in my adolescent days, and so intercourse in relationships was not a given. One evening when Karen was away from home, with her father, Julia invited me upstairs for dinner. She was a dancer, had a dancer's body, and often dressed in a leotard. I was enamored and it showed. That evening she came to my bed in the basement, and we were hooked on the fountain of sex that followed in the days that we were alone.

Danny returned after the holiday and surmised that my relationship with Julia had changed. He was angry. Moreover, Julia had revealed our situation to their therapist, who in turn informed Robert. This revelation distressed all concerned. And while the behavior of the therapist was grossly unprofessional, at least everything was out in the open. Given the untenable situation, I moved out of the house to a one-bedroom apartment on University Road, but the relationship continued and grew. Beau Fleuve was in the falls and my life was in a swirl.

A brisk autumn midday and a pervasive feeling of optimism surrounded students as they crisscrossed the bright campus of the State University of Buffalo. In the previous two years, a new science building had sprung up, an avant-garde arts center had begun to attract renowned musicians and artists, and a Nobel Laureate sat in residence in the medical school. With a growing student body and new faculty, this revitalized bastion of higher learning was on an upward trajectory, striving to take its place with the venerable Ivy League schools. A spirit of confidence infused the steps of the students. Little did they and the faculty know that the events of the day would portend a loss of hope for a generation to come.

Michel and I hurried across the campus. A Jew and a Greek, different in background and temperament, we first-born sons of immigrants were nonetheless unified in personal ambition and dedication to empirical research. As young scholars, we were training to become behavioral scientists, aiming for careers as professors—a goal they were confident was well within reach. After all, we were research assistants to a most prominent professor on campus, and our purposeful steps were taking us to complete the final condition of a study that Michel hoped to publish in a scientific research journal.

Science mattered deeply to us. The study of psychology offered the promise of understanding human behavior without the superstitions of religion, the banalities of common sense, or the so-called verities of philosophy. Science assured us that its knowledge was based on reality, not past authority. Concerted research on humans would sort out the intricacies and paradoxes of human behavior. Through controlled experiments on mental processes, the results would be analyzed, evaluated, and reported faithfully to the scientific community.

Of paramount importance to the conduct of experiments was the maintenance of pristine conditions so that the variable being studied would appear unambiguously. The invasion of extraneous or unplanned variables could contaminate the study and ruin the results. Such tainted studies were unpublishable. At this point Michel had run two experimental conditions of the current study without mishap. There was but one more study condition that required completion before the results could be tabulated.

The experiment tested the idea that authoritative feedback creates a mindset that affects the judgments people make about ambiguous information. If indefinite statements are followed by affirmation, then responses to later ambiguous statements will tend to be positive; if followed by negation, later statements will be judged as false. Michel's integrity as the source of information was crucial to the outcome of the study.

The study participants grumbled as they entered the auditorium: "Another one of those weird experiments the psych department is running. Look at those nerdy-looking grad students at the podium. They must think they're hot stuff working for Professor Bugelski."

Forms were distributed amid the smirks and snickers of participants, who were instructed to circle what they thought to be the correct True or False answer to a series of 48 ambiguously worded statements. The students' answers would be followed by Michel announcing the "correct" answers from the podium at a brisk pace of 15 seconds per question.

"The students began answering the questions, with Michel calling out the answers. "True." Pause. "False." Pause. "False." Pause.

Midway through the study, there was a commotion in the hall outside. I stepped out to investigate while Michel continued to call out responses per study protocol. I returned, whispered to Michel, and our eyes met in shocked concern. We had but one thought: "What should we do? If we let this out to the group, the experiment will be ruined."

"Ignore the hubbub. If there is any confirmation of a problem, we'll let you know," I lied to the students. "Please continue to respond to the questions."

For the next half hour, Michel continued to call out the answers in a smooth, deliberate manner, and the study proceeded in suspenseful anticipation. Any interruption would contaminate the study. At the completion of the study, a young woman left the room. She returned almost immediately; her face flushed in anger.

"You sons of bitches," she bawled. "You knew what happened but kept us in the dark to do this stupid experiment."

The participants turned to her as the blood drained from my and Michel's faces.

"President Kennedy was assassinated!"

Science reigned on the campus, but Camelot was lost to the world.

Progress toward my doctoral degree was proceeding apace. I was elected president of the Psychology Graduate Students Association, which made me a delegate to the Governance Board of graduate students for the university. The Newsomes' divorce was finalized and the house sold. By that time Danny was in graduate school at the University of Rochester, and Julia had moved into an apartment in a two-family home in Buffalo and found work as a writer in an advertising agency. Karen was in school. I felt terrible about the break-up of their marriage, but not guilty. After all, the seeds of distress in the marriage were in ground well before I appeared; professional counseling, as well as Danny's informal counseling/ had gone nowhere. Moreover, Julia and I had little contact while Robert was master of his home. Robert's decision to flee his home, leaving his dissatisfied wife with two men was unwise. Julia and I maintained separate residences, and while contact was occasional, the relationship thrived.

Occasionally, I would borrow a friend's car and drive alone to the Canadian side of Niagara Falls. In winter months the ice-capped Horseshoe Falls was spectacular. Gazing into the deep abyss, I thought about a drop of water traveling from Chicago, through the Great Lakes—Michigan, Huron, Erie—to the Beau Fleuve, over the falls into the gulf that I was staring into, wondering where my life was headed. I was in conflict with the woman I loved and my duty to my parents' wishes for me. Like Oedipus of myth, I was double minded. If I stayed with Julia, I would lose my family and identity— perhaps not irretrievably, but the wound would be deep. If I left Julia, both she and I would be irretrievably heartbroken, and I would lose a soulmate. Like Oedipus, I did nothing and courted tragedy.

B.R. Bugelski, my thesis advisor and mentor, had outlined a dissertation project for me on human verbal learning that was part of a series of experiments that he and my classmate Michel Hersen were undertaking. Known as the terror of Townsend Hall, Bugelski was highly intelligent and suffered no fools. His colleagues estimated his IQ as off the charts, close to 200. At department colloquia he would

PROFESSOR B. R. BUGELSKI

frequently pinpoint the flaw in a theory or the uncontrolled variable in a piece of research, At one colloquium, a psychiatrist from the medical school spoke proudly of the so-called Therapeutic Team, consisting of the psychiatrist, a clinical psychologist, a clinical social worker, and psychiatric nurses all working together to treat patients with behavior problems. Bugelski asked who was the captain of the team: "Was it the psychologist, the nurse?"

"No, you don't understand," sputtered the psychiatrist. "We are a team."

Bugelski retorted, "The medical profession has medicalized problems such as addiction and bad habits and taken over behavioral treatment without a skillset to change the behavior." What he meant was that psychiatry reduced behavioral problems to medicine and treated these with medication.

As Bugleski's research assistant, I conducted several verbal learning studies but did not find these of interest. On my own time, I set

GEORGE AND ALAN SIEGEL, SIGMA XI

up a small lab in the vivarium, which housed animals for research, and conducted a pilot study on fear-motivated behavior in rats. Several pilot experiments yielded positive results and I was encouraged. If a full set of experiments was conducted, the results would challenge one of the tenets of major theories of learning—namely, that fear increases fear.

One day as Bugelski was walking home, I ambushed him and asked if I could share some research findings. Excitedly, I showed him the clear results of a small sample pilot study. Bugleski's quick mind immediately seized the implications of the results, and in a stern voice said, "Do you mean that you want to do this study instead of the one I outlined for your dissertation?" With my heart in my mouth I uttered, "Yes sir, I do." He gave me a long poker-faced look, and said, "Fine, do it" and walked on home, leaving me in a state of relief. Two-weeks later, I was elected an associate member of Sigma-Xi, the national honorary science society. Bugelski was my sponsor.

Except for seminars, my formal coursework was completed, and my time was devoted to dissertation research. The object of my study was to see whether fear-motivated behavior that avoided pain could be suppressed by a threat. Behavior learning theory predicted that a threat would intensify the avoidance response. However, my experiments clearly demonstrated that a threat immediately applied would suppress the avoidance response more quickly than a delayed threat, and even more quickly than allowing the response to weaken without intervention. These findings contradicted the dominant theories of the day. Julia typed the first draft of my dissertation proposal. Interestingly, she felt that my dissertation research reflected our relationship to a large degree. My avoidance of moving our relationship to marriage was threatened by a need to adhere to my family's wishes, and as a result, action toward marriage was suppressed.

My brother, David, enrolled in courses at SUNY Buffalo and moved in with me to the apartment on University Place. Dave was a steadying presence as I worked on my dissertation research, He supported Julia and accepted our relationship, with caveats as to how the affiliation would fly with my parents. Unlike Orthodox Jewish fathers, who would hold a funeral for a son who married a shiksa, my dad would withdraw in withering silence. Both Dave and I felt that eventually mom and dad would come around to some level of acceptance. Once the semester was over, Dave returned to Chicago to accept a job at a bank.

I had submitted a brief of my research for presentation at the Midwestern Psychological Association, which was held in Chicago. Out of respect for his mentorship, I added Professor Bugelski to the paper as junior author, and the paper was accepted. The day before, I went to the meeting room and practiced giving the paper without notes. The delivery the following day was flawless, and a member of the search team for a job that I had applied for attended and offered me a research position at the University of Illinois College of Medicine in Chicago. Bugelski and a Greek American friend, George

Panagakis, attended. George's presence stimulated memories of growing up Greek in Chicago. It was both a nostalgic and unsettling experience because I felt that I was fully integrated into American society. But was I?

The dissertation proposal was approved, and the research concluded. All I had to do was write and submit the dissertation. However, my fourth year at SUNY Buffalo was ending, and I had a job offer to teach at Grinnell College in Iowa, which I accepted. A decision about the future of my relationship with Julia was coming to a head. I indicated to Julia that I was not ready to marry. Nonetheless, we agreed to drive out to Grinnell to look over the campus, located in a very rural setting. Once on the campus and meeting several faculty members, all of whom were married, we saw that living together unmarried was not possible. So, I rented an apartment for myself. We would live separately, she in Buffalo and I in Grinnell, until we could come to an agreement one way or the other. It was the kiss of death for our relationship.

The decision came on the trip back, in a seedy old hotel in Davenport, Iowa. Julia was three years older than I, and the prospect of an indefinite wait until I was ready to take marriage vows was unbearable. In an emotional exchange, she said she felt we needed to marry and start a life together right away. The ambiguity of our relationship and living apart were intolerable. Her position was understandable. What I did not understand is why she would put up with a jerk like me. I refused to marry immediately, and we returned to Buffalo in silence.

At Grinnell my classes got off to a good start. and I wrote the dissertation. Julia had typed several drafts and in the late fall, on her own initiative, came to Grinnell for a visit to review the dissertation narrative with me. The dissertation kept us together but had become symbolic of our lifeless relationship. We attended a gathering of the elite (or so they thought themselves) faculty and wives. Julia absolutely enthralled the faculty and was stunningly beautiful that evening.

She engaged in a deep conversation about music with the handsome cellist Don McCall and debated Dean Strauss about the needs of black students in an all-white college. Julia made the point that with her at my side I could become president of the college. We did not sleep together, and she left the following day with a copy of Norman Mailer's *Advertisements for Myself* in her travel bag. The highly sexual male fantasy "Time of Her Time" was her favorite piece.

Nettie Johnson prepared the final draft of my dissertation, which was submitted to the university and accepted. I arrived in Buffalo for the oral thesis defense, and it went well. Commencement was scheduled for January 1966.

Dad and I flew to Buffalo, rented a car, and spent the night at a motel. After breakfast we went to Kleinhans Music Hall for the commencement exercises. Graduate students and undergraduates together received the sheepskin in one ceremony. My classmate Alan Siegel and I shared our experiences at Beau Fleuve as we looked forward to research and teaching careers. As we lined up, I looked for Dad, but

GRADUATION, BUFFALO,, JANUARY 1966

he was not to be seen in the darkened, crowded auditorium. I wished my mom was with us, but she was at the store looking after the family business. The PhD candidates were last in line, and there were many of us. I was not sure if Dad saw me receiving the certificate, but nonetheless, afterward, he was proud.

In the foyer, Julia appeared before us and introduced herself to dad, who was cordial. He asked about her daughter, and Julia replied like the proud mother that she was. Julia was wearing an engagement ring. She was to marry a divorced professor of psychology at Hamilton University, Toronto, who played the guitar and sang to Karen and his children. Julia pulled away for a moment and wrote something on a notecard. As she departed, she pressed the card into my hand with a kiss. With a knowing look, Dad asked me if she was the woman that I had thought to marry. I remained silent. I looked at the card: *I get it, Love Julia.*

TEN

GRINNELL

The most difficult thing in life is to know yourself.
—Thales of Miletus

A s I was completing work on my doctoral dissertation, I applied for and received two offers for distinctly different careers: a fellowship in neuroscience at the University of Illinois College of Medicine, and an instructor at Grinnell College in Iowa. The former would expand my immersion in research, while the latter would involve teaching undergraduates.

The Chicago job would bring me home to my family and the circle of Greek American friends and community. Frankly, Chicago held little appeal precisely because it would bring me back to my high school Greek friendships. I was disinclined to revive my well-worn ethnic ties, preferring to keep my Greek friends at arm's length while seeking new relationships and ways of living in the broad American community.

The paradox is that the children of immigrants both value and find their ethnicity off-putting. This conflict probably works at an unconscious level to create torment but is expressed at a behavioral level. The conflict is not a rejection of ethnic identity. Rather, it is a

AUTHOR AND MERT THAYER, ELEMENTARY SCHOOL GRADUATION

dual mentality of both wanting and not wanting to be Greek. If the Chicago job had been in Boston or San Diego, I would have taken it; but, then, the Grinnell option stimulated recall of a childhood experience.

Merton Thayer was one of my best friends at Shakespeare Elementary School at 1119 East 46th Street, Chicago. We were pupils together from the third to eighth grade. Mert and I wore dusters, goggles, and moustaches side by side in the fifth-grade class rendition of *Come Away with Me Lucille in My Merry Oldsmobile.* By the standards of the day, Merton's family was well off. They lived in a large, gloomy Victorian mansion on Woodlawn Avenue, near Hyde Park, with a well-kept lawn and a barn built in horse-and-buggy days but which now contained cars.

Mert's father was the CEO of the Chicago Stock Yards, where all the live beef and pork animals from the Western states were housed for slaughter. He drove a '49 Chevy, and the family had another car that Mrs. Thayer drove to and from the South Shore Country Club. I never saw Mrs. Thayer in a house dress like my mom's; she always wore a suit, and her hair was coiffed. Mert and his younger brother, Thad, had their own rooms filled with toys, books, and games, and we spent many hours together playing. Mert's visits to my home were infrequent, mainly to attend my birthday party.

The family background was Scottish. They took pride in their frugality and sought every opportunity to trim costs. One or two days before Christmas, Mert told me. he and his dad would go to the Greek's tree stand looking for an 18-foot tree that would tower proudly, but not overly ornamented, next to the stairwell in their home. When given the price, Mert's dad would tell the shopkeeper that the tree was for the church, and the price would be lowered accordingly. As we were finishing the eighth grade, Mert told me that that he would be going to high school at the private Latin School. There he would prepare for college, his dad's college—Grinnell.

Charles Haner chaired the psychology department, housed in Goodnow Hall, when I joined the Grinnell College faculty in autumn 1965. We were a four-man department (very few women faculty in those days) and had hired an associate to manage the electronic equipment that the department used to carry out research. An Iowan by birth, Haner completed a doctorate in psychology at the University of Iowa under the prominent behavioral psychologist Kenneth Spence. Haner's classes were fully subscribed; a popular instructor, he taught personality theory, abnormal psychology, and tests and measurement. His detailed and well-worn notes were used year after year, and students in each class would reliably laugh at the same oft-told jokes.

CHARLES HANER, 1967

Haner was a mystery and a source of fascination to his colleagues. At faculty meetings he remained silent as other faculty members volubly discussed issues facing the college. Suddenly, in a whispery voice heard by all, Haner would propose a resolution that silenced the debate. The rumor of his early years at the college was that he had set up a roadside stand selling fruits and vegetables with his family in the summer months.

While college teaching was his profession, other interests occupied his energies. Grinnell Reinsurance insured the policies of other insurance companies and was the largest employer in the town. Haner had developed a questionnaire and inventory that predicted which young male drivers were a greater risk for auto accidents and which were not. The questionnaire was widely used, and Haner set up a department at the reinsurance firm for scoring and standardizing the inventory. When the *Wall Street Journal* did a front-page profile on Dr. Charles F. Haner's equities portfolio, stating that it was outperforming those of the major financial firms, his colleagues saw him as a modern-day Thales, the ancient philosopher who cornered the olive press market.[1]

Haner was a forerunner of what may be called the entrepreneurial professor. Professors write books and give lectures for royalties and honoraria, but the entrepreneur consults or starts a business for a second source of income. In essence, the benefits and achievements of academic life do not yield enough satisfaction or compensation for the entrepreneurial professor; thus, he or she applies their professional skills to another kind of challenge. On my return from Greece, Haner asked if there were any habitable unpopulated islands for sale in the Aegean. I assured him that there were. This strange query sheathed a profound dissatisfaction with academia that I detected in Haner and other faculty.

By the end of my second year of teaching, I had achieved a kind of academic success at Grinnell College. I was neither threatening nor awe-inspiring to my faculty colleagues, and my students responded favorably to my teaching. The other members of the psychology department agreed that I could handle the housekeeping duties of the department and elected me chairman.

My living arrangements consisted of an apartment in a stately colonial, built in 1863, on Sixth Avenue, about a quarter of a mile from my office in Goodnow Hall. The owners—George, a retired railway worker, and his wife, Louise Clifton—lived on the first floor; a small apartment housed an elderly widow next to the Cliftons, and upstairs were two apartments for Peter Bowman, a fellow faculty member, and me. Peter taught physics and philosophy of science. We shared a bathroom that separated the apartments, occasional dinners, and campus friends.

Being in the middle of an Iowa corn patch, Grinnell college went to great lengths to provide a cultural life on campus. The Lenox String Quartet gave concerts on a regular basis, and there were individual performances by cellist Donald McCall and brilliant lectures

MARTIN LUTHER KING CONVOCATION, 1967

by pianist Peter Hersh, as well as by other members of the quartet. From time to time the Iowa Symphony or the Goldovsky Opera Company would make an appearance on campus, and the college had a fine student orchestra. The art gallery would regularly change its shows, as did the schools' cinema studio. The college also hosted notable scholars, artists, and civic leaders. At its convocation in October, 1967, Grinnell College conferred an honorary degree on Dr. Martin Luther King, the last one he received before his assassination the following year.

King's murder triggered campus protests and urban riots against the prevailing racism, as well as the war in Vietnam in the 1960s.

Robert Kennedy's assassination on June 5th that year further disturbed the nation and intensified the antiwar movement. A year after I left Grinnell, the turmoil that gripped colleges in 1970 over the Kent State massacre led the college to cancel classes, final exams, and graduation. "An academic institution that fails to carry out its contracted purpose to its students ceases to exist." were Charles Haner's words upon his resignation. He left Iowa and settled in Escondido, California.

The laboratory was funded and set up during the first year I taught at Grinnell, and my focus centered on expanding research on the neural mechanisms of fear, and schooling undergraduates on research. However, Grinnell was a place where instruction prevailed over scholarship per se, mainly by involving students in research. Liberal arts colleges like Grinnell took seriously the education of the whole person. Nobel laureates and Pulitzer prize winners were often graduates of small liberal arts colleges. At Grinnell, Robert Noyce did experiments on integrated circuits with physics professor Grant Gale. He went to MIT, earned a PhD in physics, and later co-founded Intel, but always felt that the level of instruction at MIT did not measure up to Grant Gale's passion for physics. I taught neuroscience, learning theory, experimental psychology and involved my students in research. Many of my students went to top graduate schools and up until recent years were active contributors to the field.

Like my friend Mert Thayer, most of the students at Grinnell came from upper middle-class homes, the offspring of professional fathers and stay-at-home mothers. While not rich, they were children of privilege, somewhat pampered, with the advantages of a good education; and they were expected to do well in school and in life. I was attracted to the students from hardscrabble homes, whose families were struggling with tuition and whose preparation for college had gaps. The poorer students sought me out as an adviser and for references to graduate school. The academic achievements of my *déclassé* students were a source of personal pride.

GEORGE AT GOODENOW HALL, 1968

Grant Gale came to mind as I completed my fourth year at Grinnell, with two years as psychology department head. Grant was president of Grinnell, with the authority to administer the affairs of the college. But he elected to drop the presidency and return to his passion—teaching undergraduates. I had joined Grinnell at age 27 with a passion for teaching and research but found pleasure in administering department affairs. A good college administrator writes dropdead memoranda that covers all the bases of dissension and sticks to his point of view without antagonizing either side of an issue under discussion. This realization allowed me to refocus my career aims and reevaluate my position with the college.

In the summer of 1969, I was recruited for a teaching position at Briarcliff College in Westchester County New York, to head up the behavioral science programs—psychology and child development and education. With the refocus of career aims and with Julia out of my life, the bucolic intensity of a terrific college in a corn patch lost its appeal, added to which the long period of deprivation from Greek American culture created a thirst for my ethnic roots. New York seemed a good place to find some Greeks. The words of my college mentor came to mind when as a 20-year-old I joined a medical research center to strive my way into life as a college professor from my origins as a soda jerk in a Greek American family: "Go with the fat cats!"

Reflecting on the disorderly changes, both personal and at the college, the years at Grinnell as both fulfilling and disturbing. I conducted research on the neural basis of fear to the limits available at a liberal arts college. Two funded summer periods of postdoctoral study at MIT and the University of Washington at Seattle, respectively, enhanced my skills set in neuroanatomy and neurophysiology. However, sophisticated neuroscience experiments require a university or medical setting to fully exploit research results, along with a collegial milieu of equals to formulate new directions of study. Grinnell was neither, but I resolved to continue teaching undergraduates.

My commitment to teaching disadvantaged students would become a lifetime determination, both at Briarcliff College and Pace University. At Briarcliff the needs of students were psychological, based as it was on parental neglect of privileged young women; at Pace, the needs were didactic, based on gaps in education. My study of the human brain revealed left and right hemispheres with separate activities, with the former organizing cognition and language, and the latter focusing on emotion and creativity. While this division of brain function simplifies a complex integration of the brain, at the personal level these functions are unified to bring the individual to an awareness of what is meaningful and what is not purposeful in life.

On a personal level, with the experience of being loved and loving, I came to the realization that a life of *Mondo Cane*[2] bore no real satisfaction. Like many young men of the 1960s, I was double minded, seeking the pleasures and comforts of a soulmate but eschewing the responsibilities and commitment of a loving marriage. In a sense,

I was like a stray dog roaming the streets without a home, seeking temporary shelter with any woman who would offer sexual amenity. A loving relationship with commitment and responsibility was necessary for a useful and purposeful life.

In the 1960s liberal arts colleges experienced tragic and perhaps fatal changes to their very being. The protests of a swarming youth culture overwhelmed college administrators, who gave into the demands of students and shut down the schools. With the 1968 Paris riots and tumultuous disorder elsewhere, world culture gave in to the youth dictators, who were a mere minority. In caving to student dissent of a few, the bastions of reason and liberal learning became irrational and illiberal, and as a result, their very existence came into question. To echo Charles Haner's parting assertion, "An academic institution that fails to carry out its contracted purpose to its students ceases to exist." Of course, colleges and universities carried on and continued to offer instruction, but without the authority of the years prior to the riots. The liberal ideal of rational debate ceased to exist in academia beset by mob rule.

When I asked James Stauss, the dean of the college, about Merton Thayer's time at Grinnell, he told me that Mert flunked out, was given a reprieve, reinstated, and flunked out again. This was surprising and unexpected. Perhaps the advantages of a comfortable upbringing and an alumnus Dad had limits.

NOTES

1. Somehow, through observation of the heavenly bodies, Thales concluded that there would be a bumper crop of olives. He raised money to place a hold on the olive presses of Miletus and Chios, so that when the harvest was ready, he was able to let out the presses at a rate that brought him considerable profit,

thereby answering his critics' taunts: If you're so smart, why aren't you rich?

2. *A Dog's World,* 1962 documentary consisting of a series of travelogue vignettes providing a glimpse into cultural practices throughout the world intended to shock or surprise.

ELEVEN

WILD BERRIES
AT DELPHI

One had a pretty face,
and two or three had charm,
but charm and face were in vain
Because the mountain grass
Cannot but keep the form
Where the mountain hare has lain.
—from "Memory" by W.B. Yeats

During a touching scene in Ingmar Bergman's film *Scenes from a Marriage,* the characters, Marianne (Liv Ulman) and Johan (Erland Josephson), lie blissfully embraced on their bed, secure in their union—just as Odysseus and Penelope joyfully entwined in their great rooted bed on his return to Ithaka. Most of us seek a soulmate to face life's demands. Such was I, a soulmate seeker, as I packed copies of Edith Hamilton's *Mythology,* and John Fowles' *The Magus,* hardly rational companions for a first journey to Greece, my parent's homeland.

GEORGE AND GARGOYLES, NOTRE DAME CATHEDRAL, PARIS

It was a circuitous grand tour from London to Goteborg, where I picked up the two-door Volvo sedan I had purchased, and from there drove on to Hamburg, Amsterdam, Brussels, Paris, Montreux, Milan, and Rome. From there my sister, Peggy (Panayiota), and I boarded a car ferry at Brindisi. It was summer, and as teachers we had the luxury of ten weeks to travel. Greece was our destination, and since this was to be my introduction to the land of contrasts and my sister was to make it her residence, we eagerly boarded the boat for the trip to Patras.

It was onboard that we met. Judith was on a grand tour herself and after Greece had scheduled a visit to Venice. A copy of.D.F. Kitto's *The Greeks* peered out of her travel case, a rational choice. She had completed her graduate work in oceanography at UC Santa Barbara, and I had received a graduate degree in psychology at SUNY at Buffalo and was teaching at Grinnell College. As freshly minted PhDs, our shared experiences working our way through grad school bonded us. Long years of study and research washed away as the boat cruised into the Adriatic. Our attraction was immediate and poignant.

Judith was an American girl with a lithe swimmer's frame, of quiet disposition, and open to new experience. She was a conscientious, authoritative woman, well-read beyond her scientific training. We understood that our developing friendship was fleeting and used the evening onboard to share and discuss all we cared to reveal to each other. We were kindred souls intent on exploring Greece in the few days that we were to be together.

When we entered Patras harbor, I exchanged hotel addresses with Judith, who had already arranged to travel to Athens, and we resolved to meet.

Once in Athens, my sister and I were embraced by loving aunts, uncles, cousins, and various other family members. "Of course, you must come to the house for lunch or dinner," said Theia Katerino. Everyone will be there." On then to Theia Ellie, who made the same request for a visit, as did the others: "Please plan to come to Theio Gioryo and Theia Matina," The cascade of invitations continued as I made a concerted effort to postpone family visits so I could explore the Acropolis and Benaki Museum with my new friend.

Judith and I also motored from Athens 60km (37 miles) to Cape Sounion, a peninsula on the southernmost portion of Attica to the east, facing the Aegean and the Cyclades. As we traveled, Judith revealed that she envied me, a tenure track professor with a research program and grants at a top liberal arts college. More than anything she aspired to do research and teach at a university. She had several offers for university posts but had decided to postpone an academic career.

We scrambled up the promontory to the Temple of Poseidon, the sea god, and found the graffiti of Lord Byron's name, which he had etched into the base. We were thrilled by the expanse of the seas. Psychologist Abraham Maslow would say that we had an oceanic experience, a sense of oneness with the universe. On the road back to Athens, we ate at a roadside inn and found an empty beach a few kilometers down the road. We had brought towels and swimsuits and threw ourselves into the ocean. Judith swam fishlike, without breaking or splashing the water. We dried ourselves in the afternoon sun, kissed, but wisely, did not make love on the deserted beach.

The following day, Judith and I met at Syntagma Square in the early morning, had a Nescafe and brioche, and decided to take a day trip to Delphi, perhaps to consult the oracle. Negotiating the maze of narrow streets crammed with motorbikes, cars, and pedestrians in Athens poses a challenge for even the most experienced driver. Once on the open road, the 181 km trip (100 miles) on paved and unpaved two-lane roads took four hours. (Currently the trip on superhighway 1 is just over two hours.) We chatted about the terrain, the crucifix memorials marking auto deaths, our favorite music. We listened to popular Greek songs on the radio, interspersed with periods of silence that betrothed our thoughts. We arrived at Delphi, the ancient site of the temple and oracle of Apollo, shortly after noon. Summer tourism had not taken root, so we had the place to ourselves.

The Charioteer greeted our entry to the Delphi Museum—a bronze statue of a young man in a long robe driving a chariot and holding the reins in his right hand. The left arm was missing. The charioteer's feet were bare and crafted with a high degree of detail. The statue's life-like appearance was accentuated by the tilt of the body and head slightly toward the right. Dedicated 2500 years ago as an offering to the god Apollo for a chariot race victory, the Charioteer of Delphi has religious significance as a votive but is also a symbol of competition in the ancient Greek games, as well as the quest for *areté* (excellence) in Greek life. Judith wondered whether the ancient Greeks valued competition more than beauty.

Delphi lies in the territory of Phocis on the steep lower slope of Mount Parnassus, about 10 km (6 miles) from the Gulf of Corinth. The temple sanctuary was a large, roughly rectangular area enclosed by a wall. A sacred way lined with monuments and treasuries wound

GEORGE ON THE ROAD TO DELPHI

through the sanctuary to the Temple of Apollo itself, which housed the Delphic oracle in a chamber at the rear. It was there that municipalities and individuals sought the favors bestowed by the god. Hand in hand, Judith and I strode through the existing temple site, which includes only the foundation, some steps, and a few columns remaining from the structure built in the 4th century BC.

We climbed to the highest elevation of the grounds, overlooking the sanctuary of Apollo, and marveled at the view of a glorious world in ruin. To the north, the Stadium of Delphi, with views of the archeological site, was built on the slope of a mountain, and to the South a wall was constructed that formed the seating for about 6500 spectators. Various athletic field and track competitions as well as musical events were held at the stadium's sprinting track—177.5 meters (582 feet) long and 25.5 m (83 feet) wide. We approached the starting line gingerly, checked out the length of the running track, and toed the marble sprinting blocks. Judy impishly cast a challenge, "You wanna race to the end?" Before I could reply, the fleet-footed Amazon darted forward, skirt flowing, and the plodding academic followed, ego in certain jeopardy of defeat. Of course, Judith won the race, and we retired to a copse of cool trees at the end of the running track.

We were famished and discovered a blaze of wild berries nearby. Between us, our practical knowledge of the difference between poisonous berries and edible berries was sufficient to determine that these blueberries were indeed fit for consumption, and we dug in. Soon fingers, faces, and clothing were basted with blueberry juice, and we proceeded to smear each other with the stuff. It was a moment of childish delight that I will ever cherish. It was also a moment of Edenic innocence that we sealed with the sweetest kiss.

From Delphi we drove back to Athens, with my companion in solitary silence for much of the journey. Like Judith, I had qualms about our situation. I was double minded like many young men in the 1960s. I sought the pleasures and comforts of a soulmate but was not interested in the responsibilities and commitment of a relationship. Like the tragic myth of Oedipus, who both believed and disbelieved that he had committed the disastrous act of slaying his father and marrying his mother, I both believed and disbelieved in marriage. Instead, I casually flowed from one romance to another without purpose—the Grecian tragedy of missing the mark.

We stopped at a seaside restaurant for a farewell dinner that was largely uneaten. Judith was boarding a ship the next day bound for Venice. She told me that from Venice she would travel to Vienna to meet her mother. Then she and her mother were to fly to Cape Town, where her fiancé had arranged for their marriage. We agreed to meet the next morning to say goodbye.

Athens was coming to life as pedestrians, cyclists, and automobiles made their daily rounds. At the terminal for Piraeus-bound buses, we stood in sad solidarity, with the inevitable parting hovering before us. "Give me your address, I want to stay in touch with you," she said. Which I did. But she never wrote.

TWELVE

A PLACE FOR GOD

We may ignore, but we can nowhere evade the presence of God
—C.S. Lewis

Our move to 47th street, Chicago brought me to the St. Ambrose Elementary School on Ellis Avenue a few blocks from our apartment. I was enrolled in the first grade; A requirement was weekly attendance at mass, and morning confession with the attending priest. We lined up before the church confessional and one by one unloaded the sins of the previous week. "How many times did you lie to your parents?" A random number was pulled from the air. "Say 30 Hail Marys. How often did you curse? Say 40 Hail Marys." And so it went until I was released and the next pupil went into the confessional. It was apparent to the teachers and clergy that I was an ill fit for Catholic education and so the requirement to attend Catechism classes was dropped. In Nicos Kazantzakis's *Zorba the Greek* is a comment that the deceased French prostitute, Bouboulina, was not given an Orthodox funeral because she crossed herself with four fingers, while Greeks use only three; I was equally clueless about Catholicism. Just as I was to enter the third grade, the nuns of St. Ambrose expelled me, to the astonished grief of my mother. As we passed the school on the way to Shakespeare Public School. my mother implored me to plead to the nuns to reinstate me. No way: I was resolute.

My first clear memory of being in a Greek Orthodox church dates back to 1947 at the entry way of St Constantine and Helen Church on 61st and Michigan Avenue, Chicago.[1] It was a sunny summer day, perhaps on the Feast of the Dormition of the Panagia, and men and boys stood outdoors, chatting, smoking, and engaging in horseplay, while the women, girls, and the priest, Fr. Mark Petrakis (the father of author Harry Mark Petrakis) were in the church. I was with the men and boys, more as an observer than a participant. At the time, a raffle for a new car, a Tucker '48 (an automobile conceived by Preston Tucker and briefly produced in Chicago that year) was being held to raise money to build a church on 74th and Stony Island Avenue. The prospects of a new Byzantine Church modeled after the Hagia Sophia of Constantinople enthralled the parish. However, like most major construction projects, the funding depended on the largesse of a few large doners. Fortunately, the parish had several wealthy sponsors—for instance, Pierre De Mets, who with others provided the funds for an orderly completion of the structure.

After the footings were laid, Divine Liturgy was conducted in the cavernous basement as the outer shell of concrete blocks was being laid. I mentioned horseplay of the lads. During one Sunday service, Demetrios Stevens climbed up a tier of concrete on which the uppermost block was uncemented; he and the block fell over 20 feet, with the block crushing his leg. No doubt he was testing his climbing skill, much as rock climbers test themselves against sheer mountain walls. Demetrios did not return to church, and I never learned of his condition. However, His accident was a cautionary tale for me about taking unnecessary risks.

Greeks have an aversion to risk and take measures to avoid uncertainty. According to Hofstede's Cultural Dimensions (a framework used to understand the differences in culture across countries), Greek culture has the highest possible score for uncertainty avoidance. This finding indicates that Greeks seek stability and security in their dealings with their culture and with each other. Greeks will take steps in advance to carefully plan an event, be it a dinner, baptism, wedding, or any of the many proceedings that make up social and business life. For a family dinner, much thought is given to the menu, and last-minute change creates distress. Business practice places the family, rather than outsiders, in charge of running the business. In Greece and to a lesser extent in the U.S., most businesses are family owned and few are structured around an impersonal corporation, thereby reducing risk and uncertainty. What is the basis for this powerful trait?

Certainly, centuries of occupation by the Ottoman tyranny based in Constantinople contributed to a culture without local civic leadership. Accordingly, in the rural regions like Mani, Laconia, and Epirus, the extended family governed and set standards of personal, and group conduct as opposed to entities and domains outside of the family. Such family governance reduced risk and the uncertainly posed by the larger culture. Another factor was the constancy of the Holy Orthodox Church. While the family governed the hearth, God governed the heart. The church mediated man's relationship to God, set as it was in the church calendar. For instance, the 40 days before Pascha (Easter) is a prayerful period of fasting and preparation of mind and body for the resurrection of Christ. Moreover, other fasting periods, the mid-August Dormition of the Panagia and the weeks before Christmas, further reinforce spiritual connection to the Deity. During most of the year Wednesdays and Fridays are days of fasting from meat and spirits. The regularity and constancy of the church calendar reduced uncertainty. Then each Sunday, the Orthodox are called to church for the Divine Liturgy.

Seated in the children's section at the side of the church, and at an appointed time after Holy Communion, we marched out of the Divine Liturgy to the classroom building which also served as the Koreas School during the week. Sunday school classes were

PETER, SOPHIA, GEORGE, PEGGY, AND DAVID
IN FRONT OF SAINTS CONSTANTINE AND HELEN
GREEK ORTHODOX CHURCH, CHICAGO

conducted by the pious, Mrs. Parthenia Thalassinou (the feminine of her husband's surname) Her husband, Themis Thaalassinos taught also, and they were a model Orthodox Christian couple working in the Lord's vineyard. [In our first years as a married couple Doulie and I performed similar Sunday School duties.] The faith and teachings of Mrs. Thalassinou moved me deeply. I thought that she was the embodiment of the Panayia and hung on her every word; Sunday School class was a place for God.

Pascha was among the few times we attended church as a family. For my dad, building up the family business was central to his efforts, so the store was open regular hours on Sundays and Holidays. At times mother would join us at church, but often the morning ritual of prayer and censing the icons at our home sufficed for her. Like most parishioners, we were not regular communicants. However, each month mom would donate a few dollars to the church for the icon of the Panagia. She had accumulated enough to cover the costs of the icon but was told that the icon had been given to a wealthy family to be named as donor. Such are the politics of giving at a place for God.

Holy Confession was mandated for the altar boys and pupils of the Sunday School during Holy Week. The priest would hear our sins (hamartias) face to face, read a prayer of forgiveness, and dismiss us for the next sinner, much as had the priest at St. Ambrose. As a youngster, I found this sacrament of atonement expiated my concerns over my shortcomings, real and imagined. It was a cleansing experience, and I felt somehow purified until about age 15, when, sadly, I discarded the image of Christ and Holy Confession.

Much of my confusion centered on the freshman high school science class. The instructor, Mrs. Minerva Constatinides, discussed Darwin's theory of evolution as the likely explanation for the origin of the human species. She was not critical of the idea of God as the originator of the universe; nor did she discuss a conflict with religion. Accordingly, my attention merely turned to science as explaining the cosmos, and religion played less and less in my thinking about human existence and being. The very vastness of the universe and the idea of the Big Bang as its origin rejected the idea of a creator as the source of its existence. I continued in this line of thinking through all my school years –high school, college, graduate school, and post-doctoral fellowships. A place for God was nearby, but I was missing.

GREEK IDENTITY AND THE ORTHODOX CHURCH

What role does the church play in preserving Greek ethnic and cultural identity in the United States? Perhaps no institution conserved Greek identity more than the Greek Orthodox Church. Immigrants draw on the social, cultural, and spiritual resources from their home country to maintain their identity as they seek to integrate into their new environment. With integration, the settlers learn the language, customs, and ways of life of their adopted country but struggle to maintain their home country ties. For some émigrés, it was fellowship with others from the same region where the same Greek dialect is spoken. During the early immigration days of the 1900s, individuals from the same village or district bonded. For instance, in Chicago the immigrants from the Sparta region founded the Spartan Society of which my dad, Peter, was a member. Such fellowship reinforced links to shared experiences, cuisine, and personal history but also afforded information on jobs, housing, citizen requirements, and the news from home. The Greek Orthodox Church was the place for worship where Greek was spoken, faith was reinforced, and where the expression of Hellenic identity was welcome. It was also a venue for making friends, teaching youth, and a marriage market.

In the 1963 film *America, America,* written, directed, and produced by Elia Kazan, young Stavros Topouzoglou (Stathis Giallelis), who lost his family's fortune, is brought to the Greek Orthodox Cathedral in Constantinople by his uncle. to be seen by and to see a young marriageable woman from a wealthy family. Seated in the men's and women's sections, respectively, the young people surreptitiously glance at each other during the service. Later they meet in a chaperoned setting and become engaged. Indeed, this bravura performance is highly desired by many Greek parents for their young marriageable, daughters and sons, whether at a church, summer camp, youth program, university club, or church dance. Value is placed on common religion and a communal ethnicity. The church is not only the venue for such betrothals but holds the matrix of shared growing up experiences that bring young people together. At summer camp Ionian Village, sponsored by the Greek Orthodox Archdiocese, youngsters from widely different regions of the U.S. discover highly similar parental attitudes on dating, curfews, friendships, appearance, and the values of higher education and their Hellenic heritage. In summary, the Greek Orthodox Church sustained Greek identity through it youth programs and Hellenic Schools.

THE SIXTIES

Youth culture saturated the sixties; it pervaded dress, music, sexuality, politics, marriage, social attitudes, and personal appearance. The 1960s was one of the most tumultuous and divisive decades in the U.S., marked by the civil rights movement, the Vietnam War and antiwar protests, second wave feminism, political assassinations and the emerging generation gap. John Kennedy's election as president kicked off the decade with his call to youth to serve their country through the Peace Corp. Kennedy's assassination in November 23, 1963 was the watershed event that divided youth from the U.S. culture, and separated the 1960s from the ethos and mores of previous decades. One impactful casualty of the decade was religion.

Scholars of domestic life have chronicled the decline of the family in the United States that coincides with a decline in religion. The religiosity index, a measure of interest in religion and attendance of religious services, shows a decline in religion beginning in 1962. Based on over 400 surveys that measured congregation membership, attendance, worship, prayer, feelings toward religion, the multivariate graph below shows the decline.

This index tells the story of the rise and fall of religious activity. During the post-war, baby-booming 1950s, there was a revival of religion. Indeed, some at the time considered it a third great awakening" (Grant, 2014). With the death of John Kennedy, came the societal changes of the 1960s, which included questioning religious institutions, government, the economy, military, marriage, and belief in God. The decline stabilized at the end of the 1960s for about two decades, then continued for the next 20 years. Religion was hit hard, along with social behaviors associated with a religious life, including respect for chastity, the sanctity of marriage, the value of family and social cohesion. The decline heralded a forfeiture of God-centered values. Paradoxically, the Greek Orthodox Church grew during the 1960s and 1970s, and new churches were established.

My personal situation followed a decline in religion and scruples from the 1950s until 1969. The 1966 film *Alfie* characterizes the behavior of young men at the time and, to some extent, mine. Set in London, *Alfie* features Michael Caine as a self-centered playboy bent on promiscuity. After impregnating his girlfriend, he takes off on vacation. He continues his life of womanizing, but he can't hide forever. Tragedy strikes, and he is forced to consider his life. The final image of the film shows Alfie at night, on a deserted street, walking alone with a stray dog stepping ahead of him. As a young man of the times, I did not discard my virginity until I was 23 years old, yet I regret the shallowness of my actions that followed and the lack of seriousness, so necessary to a well-ordered life.

The sixties offered a Playboy cornucopia of sex: Get as much as you can. This narcissistic egocentric commerce between men and women damaged stable relations between the sexes and undermined commitment to relationship and marriage. I believe the sixties led to less respect and trust between men and women that bled into higher divorce rates and a breakup of the family structure. But for me, there was the prospect of redemption, not that it was deserved.

C.S. Lewis thrusts Christ, the diver, into the bottom of a brackish water hole within the human debris of Satan's handiwork, and amidst the slime of sin, embraces a soul and brings him to the surface. I was that soul. Unexpectedly, Christ found me in a college seminar room, set aside for a small group of professors to have lunch and discuss the first 18 verses of John 1 of the Gospel. We attended an entire semester of weekly meetings for a discussion of God—for me a place for God. John Crossett, professor of classics, led the group through the meanings of "In the origin there was the Logos and the Logos was present with God, and the Logos was god (Εν άρχή ἦν ὁ λόγος καί ὁ λόγος ἦν πρός τόν θεόν, καί θεός ἦν ὁ λόγος). "John 1 elegantly reveals the theology of the person of Christ, and in the 20th chapter in which Thomas addresses Jesus as My Lord and My GOD, (ὁ κύριός μου καί ὁ θεός μου) shows God and Jesus were one. These signs have been recorded so that we might have faith that Jesus is the Anointed Son of God, and that in having faith you might have life in his name" (Hart, 2017). The revelation of the unity God and Jesus came streaming forth from my years of reciting the Nicene Creed, church worship, catechism, mother's votive candle at the iconostasis. But now it had a place in my heart.

Was there a sweeping change in my outlook and behavior as a result of this apotheosis of faith? Certainly not at Grinnell College. I remained the worldly, striving careerist, seeking to achieve a place for myself in academe, improving my teaching, writing articles, serving on committees, and chairing the psychology department. While I took a sincere interest in the Holy Bible and books on religion, these activities were at an intellectual level and did little to move me closer to Christ. However, the seeds of faith were re-planted.

After four years at Grinnell College, the move from Iowa to New York opened the opportunity for regular church worship and church service in 1969. I contacted Fr. Robert Stephanopoulos at the well-appointed Church of Our Saviour in suburban Rye; his conducting of the Divine Liturgy and thought-provoking sermons were outstanding and the management of the church progressive. Fr. Bob became my Father Confessor, and we remain friends. I began regular attendance at the worship services and continue to follow Christ.

What struck me about the church in Rye was the absence of icons on the walls and interior dome, which typically appear in Greek Orthodox churches, proclaiming the glory of God and the holy saints. An icon screen of Christ and the Theotokos separated the narthex from the altar, but there were no icons elsewhere. This feature made

REV. ROBERT STEPHANOPOULOS, 1964

the church look more like a Protestant than an Orthodox church. The absence of icons did not appear to disturb the parishioners. In fact, many found the absence of the icons restful and pleasing. One could only ponder what was appealing about this austerity. Eventually, over the years in bits and patches, icons appeared and covered the entire church.

Also, I wondered why *Saviour* in the name of the church was spelled with a "u" in the British manner. This spelling remained a mystery until I happened on a novel by Nicholas Gage (of Eleni fame), *The Bourlotas Fortune*, a fictionalized account based loosely on the rise of Greek ship-owning families in the last century. Gage mentions the arrival in New York of a coterie of Greek ship owners from embattled Britain during World War II. They traveled by a neutral Panamanian ship seeking refuge from bombed-out London and a secure place to conduct their business of shipping goods for the Allies cause. According to Gage, some of the immigrants were welcomed to Rye by the film tycoon Spiro Skouras. They settled in homes and retained their British ways. Here the Gage account ends. In the early 1950s, with their families growing the need for a nearby place of worship became evident and idea of establishing a church in Rye took root.

Among these Greek Britons, energetic ship owner Costas Lemos took leadership of the parish project and invited other maritime executives to join the parish council, many of whom were also from England. Once permission to establish a Church in Rye was obtained in 1957 from the Archdiocese, Lemos convinced David Rockefeller of the Chase bank to make a loan without personal collateral for the purchase of property on Westchester Avenue that housed the Harmony Estate. The mansion and parish house were the core, along with 10 acres of pristine property. Lemos then engaged Stephen Lyras and John Kokkins to prepare an architectural scheme for a rotunda style church without fee. When the papers for the loan were drawn up, Saviour was spelled the British way and so remained.

Fr. Robert suggested I join him and his wife, Presbytera Nicki, for the church's annual Candlelight Ball at the Westchester Country Club. This annual event raised money to close the gap between dues collections and the deficit. It was a sparkling event, with many from New York City making the trip to suburban Harrison, NY. All duded up in rented tuxedo, I arrived at the club and was introduced by Fr. Robert to a lovely young woman named Doulie Pappas, who was standing under a palm tree, reminiscent of one of Paul Gauguin's Tahitian paintings. It was a set-up by the matchmaker priest and good friends, Ted and Maro Tsagaris. Not surprisingly Doulie and I were seated at the Tsagaris table. However, the attraction between us was strong, and I immediately knew that I wanted to be with her. After a couple of barely eaten courses, I whispered to Doulie that we take off, and she agreed with a wink. Surreptitiously, we left the ball, went to a club, and talked for hours over drinks. When I dropped her off at her home in the early morning, as she stepped on the stair her ballgown rose over her delicate right ankle, like Persephone's. I knew that she was someone that I wanted to get to know better. She evinced a graceful quality that made people want to be with her and a spirituality that gave comfort.

Her Greek parents met me on our first date. To the consternation of her stepmother, Pauline, Doulie puckishly introduced me as a Jewish guy. But no one was fooled. Pauline had a full account from Maro Tsagaris of our furtive escape from the ball and who I was. When we arrived at Doulie's home that evening, a plate of baklava was on the kitchen table for me. The fish was hooked. From then on Doulie and I saw each other almost every day. Doulie was a special education teacher, but was family oriented, deeply religious, and respectful and loving of others. She met my parents in Chicago, who embraced and loved her. We became engaged a year later and married soon after.

DOULIE, 1971

So traditional, yet so in keeping, ultimately, with who we were and with whom we were fated to fall in love. In our years together, she has always been Doulie, a real person—not merely my idea of Doulie.

In our house-hunting days, Doulie and I were shown a well-situated home on a level plot with many attractive features: up-to-date kitchen and baths, good-sized bedrooms, plenty of living space for dining and socializing. The family had moved out and had taken the furniture, so we could only fantasize about how they lived. As we walked through the house, the real estate agent pointed out a small room with ambient lighting off the sun parlor and said, "This room was the chapel. Of course, you can always use it as a TV room."

The chapel? We had never seen a home with an entire room devoted exclusively to prayer. Italian palazzos often had a chapel with an altar, a crucifix, a statue of the Virgin Mary, but this was not at all typical in the United States. I imagined a room with pews and a cross, with the family of this pious household going into the chapel for their morning prayers or retreating there in the evening to pray before bedtime. Perhaps they invited a priest or pastor to conduct prayer services, or possibly it was a sanctuary for meditation and soul searching. It was a place for God.

Certainly, there is a need for a place to retreat from the cares and "noise" of the world to be with God. In Orthodox homes, a place is set aside for icons of Christ, the Theotokos, a patron saint, and perhaps the wedding crowns. My mother, Sophia, kept a votive candle burning day and night over the iconostasis, displayed prominently in the hallway of her home for all to see. Our own home has icons, without a votive lamp, over the doorway inside our bedroom for only Doulie and me to see. The contrast speaks of different worlds and different mentalities, but the need for a place for God remains unchanged, a need that can be fulfilled in a school, church, or one's home.

Early in the year our parish priest, Fr. Elias Villis, will invite us to open our homes for house blessings. He will arrive at an appointed time, and we will set up a temporary place to pray, replete with an icon, a votive light, and burning incense. After the prayers, he will sprinkle holy water throughout every room in the house and on its residents. We feel the home is sanctified after a house blessing and look forward to the year ahead with that confidence. However, have we made a place for God?

St. Basil offers this guidance, "When you look at the sky and the beauty of the stars, throw yourself at God's feet and adore Him who in His wisdom has arranged things in this way. Similarly, when the sun goes down and when it rises, when you are asleep or awake, give thanks to God, who created and arranged all things for your benefit, to have you know, love and praise their Creator."

It matters not whether we set aside a room for God or a chapel or iconostasis. What matters is that we place God at the center our lives. A physical setting certainly is a powerful facilitator of regular prayer and stands as a reminder of our need to be with God. But our prayers are heard wherever we are.

NOTE

1. The origin of the Saints Constantine and Helen Greek Orthodox Parish began with services held at a rented hall at 63rd and Woodlawn Ave. It was at a meeting held on April 25, 1909, that 350 people voted to establish an independent church dedicated to Saints Constantine and Helen. The first church was built at 61st and Michigan and opened its doors in October of 1910.

THIRTEEN

THE AFTERLIFE OF A NAME

No man is rich enough to buy back his past.
—Oscar Wilde

Death is a mystery. What follows death, the afterlife, if it exists, an even a more profound mystery. The idea of an afterlife is offered to allay our ignorance or bolster our hope about what may happen after our breath becomes air. Carl Jung believed that the afterlife myth resides in the collective unconscious, that aspect of our consciousness embedded in lore that is shared across cultures.

According to Jung, "Myth is the natural and indispensable stage between unconscious and conscious cognition . . . a knowledge of a special sort, knowledge in eternity without reference to the here and now, not couched in the language of the intellect.[1] Through myth, an understanding of the afterlife becomes possible.

Myths of the afterlife hold that the immortal soul leaves the body for a place sometimes called heaven and other times Valhalla, a place in Norse mythology that received the souls of fallen heroes. Whether the soul is fully conscious or holds a fragment of consciousness after we die is unknown. But the idea is that an aspect of the person exists after death.

To quote a verse from the Hávamál (The Sayings of the High One), the pre-Christian poem attributed to Odin, "cattle die, the family dies, you'll die yourself, but one thing that never dies is the name the man leaves behind him.[2,3]

The repute a man leaves behind him is captured in *The Iliad* as the warrior hero Achilles contemplates a prophesy about his demise and his place in eternity:

My mother Thetis a moving silver grace,
Tells me two fates sweep me on to my death.
If I stay here and fight I'll never return home,
But my glory will be undying forever.
If I return home to my dear fatherland
My glory is lost but my life will be long.[4]

A long life, or a name that brings enduring fame? Indeed, Achilles' name lives in perpetuity as the warrior's warrior, ever victorious in battle, whether or not he lives on in the underworld.

But what about us ordinary folk, those of us without any particular glory to celebrate? Is the one thing that never dies the name the decedent leaves behind? The idea of our reputation continuing to exist beyond our existence as living human beings is a kind of afterlife.

I was thunderstruck when a name from the past popped up to invade my present day. My computer had locked me out of an account, and I was prompted to come up with a new password. The admonition was not to use any past password. I scanned my crib sheet of passwords and was stuck. I had to come up with an all-new password and had exhausted my supply of meaningful (to me), easily remembered passwords. I racked my mind to come up with some-

THE AFTERLIFE OF A NAME

thing different—at least six letters, upper and lower case, and at least one number. Strangely, the name of a college friend came to mind. So I typed in Panagakis55 and retyped it as prodded, and immediately my brokerage account opened. Never before had I used anyone's last name as a password.

George Panagakis and I attended college together, and the number 55 referred to the year of our graduation, 1955, from different high schools. In addition to our first names, Panagakis and I had shared the same group of friends. But over the years we had little contact and lived separate existences—he in Chicago and I in New York. We were not close and shared few mutual interests, but he was a serious man with an avid interest in politics. We spoke last about three years ago. We stopped exchanging Christmas cards once Alzheimer's disease had taken hold of him.

About an hour after I changed my password to Panagakis55, I received this e-message from a mutual friend: *Hello, George, our friend George Panagakis left us yesterday.* What an amazing happening! The news of his death stunned me coming as it did shortly after the password was posted. His passion for politics came to mind. Was it a chance coming together of discrete events or was it a paranormal event? A mystery!

Such experiences reinforce the notion of an afterlife. Perhaps the belief in an afterlife is not so absurd after all. Premonitions are common happenings over a large sample of individuals. Most of us, or someone we know, has had a premonition or a dream of an event that happened later just as our mind experienced it. Occasionally, some of us communicate remotely with another person distantly in time or space—perhaps a dream conversation with the departed or the awareness of an absent friend who relates to us poignantly.[5]

Paradoxically, atheists, agnostics, and the non-religious cling to the idea that some aspect of their being will persist after death. For atheists who espouse a wholly material universe, this confidence in the afterlife is perplexing. If matter is the essence of the person and consciousness depends on a functioning brain and body, then what is the nature of the "us" that perseveres after death when brain and body are returned to dust. Perhaps only our reputation?

I thought of my erstwhile friend. George had taken his last breath, pronounced dead by the hospice orderly who attended him in the last hours. After a respectful period of mourning, his remains would be taken to the crematorium and the ashes scattered as he requested. Several weeks later George's family would gather for a memorial service, recounting those endearing singular qualities that made him the special person that he was. Refreshments would be served afterwards, and the conversation would turn to other topics. Weeks later probate would be completed, the will read, assets distributed, clothing donated to Goodwill, and special personal items—books, jewelry, artwork—given to family and friends who wished to have them. With time his possessions would become theirs, and his identity with the items would dissipate. Later someone would recall the classmate who ran for president of the class of 1955: "What was his name?"

REFERENCES

1. Jung, C. (1959). "The concept of the collective unconscious" (1936) in *Collected works* (Vol. 9.I, p. 42). Editors' note: Originally given as a lecture to the Abernethian Society at St. Bartholomew's Hospital, London, on October 19, 1936, and

2. Ferguson, R. (2017). *Scandinavians: In search of the soul of the North* (p. 64). Overlook Press.

3. Another version of the Odin Hávamál reference (Oliver Bray, trans.; D. L. Ashliman, ed.) published in the Hospital's *Journal*, XLIV (1936/37), pp. 46–49, 64–66.

Cattle die and kinsmen die,
thyself too soon must die,
but one thing never, I ween, will die—
fair fame of one who has earned.

4. Homer. *The Iliad* (1970), Book IX, p. 216. (Robert Fitzgerald, trans.). Anchor Books, Doubleday.
5. Zimmar, G. (2017). "Mind at large," *Journal of Humanistic Psychiatry*, 5(4), pp. 23–26.

FOURTEEN

EN PASSANT

Perched on the loftiest throne in the world,
we are still sitting on our own behind.
—Michel de Montaigne

H is opponent smiled and took a thoughtful puff on his Meer-schaum, "Max, this is the first time in several weeks that you have come up even with me on the chessboard."

Max picked up the well-worn pieces and returned them to the frayed cardboard box. He knew that his opponent would not have time to finish the game and that his departure was imminent.

A refugee from the Nazi regime, Max's chess partner had resided in Princeton for 20 years. He had been a professor at the University of Berlin. But when Hitler assumed power, he renounced his German citizenship, traveled to the United Sates and established residence. In contrast to Germans, he found, "Americans friendly, optimistic, energetic, and without envy."[1]

Before the Great Depression, Max Lerner had been a successful clothing manufacturer. However, economic vicissitudes had left him penniless and without his business. For a while he and his wife lived with her parents until Max could pull together enough money to purchase a stationery store at 82 Nassau Street. Faculty from Princeton University often dropped by for an egg cream, the *New York Times*, or a package of cigarettes.

In passing the shop from his home on 112 Mercer Street, his opponent had initially dropped in to pick up a package of Revelation tobacco. He noticed a chessboard with the pieces in place for a game. As he paid his bill, the customer suggested, "Perhaps we can play a friendly game?"

"Whenever you would like. I would be honored," Max replied.

A tournament began at the shop in earnest in the weeks that followed. Max's opponent had a solitary request: that the games be played in the back of the shop, away from the prying eyes of faculty or students. After all, he was an eminent physicist at the Institute for Advanced Studies, and Max was a mere shopkeeper. It would be unseemly for them to be seen in competition. Over time they developed a rapport, and Max felt that he could ask personal questions about his opponent's religious beliefs as they played the game.

"Pick. Right hand or left." Max selected White, and the play began, appropriately enough, with the Vienna Game opening.[2]

White: P-K4: "In the beginning God created Heaven and the Earth."[3] Would you agree?"

Black: P-K4: "I want to know how god created this world. The rest is mere details."[4]

White: N-QB3: "And the Spirit of God moved on the face of the waters.

Black: N-KB3: "I am not interested in this or that phenomenon, in the spectrum of this or that element. I want to know his thoughts."[5]

White: P-B4: "For His thoughts, do you pray to God?"

Black: P-Q4: "Do you mean Yahweh?"

White: BPxP: "Yes, I mean Yahweh."

Black: NxP: "Well, if you mean a personal god, certainly not![6] The idea of a personal god is an anthropological concept that I am unable to take seriously."[7]

White N-B3: "God was certainly personal when He addressed Adam and Eve in Genesis and the Prophets throughout the Torah."

Black B-K2: "The word "god" is for me nothing more than the expression and product of human weaknesses, the Bible a collection of honourable but still primitive legends which are nevertheless pretty childish."[8]

"Biblical exegesis of the Torah reveals a coherent and consistent account of creation."

"No interpretation, no matter how subtle, can change this for me."[9]

White: P-Q4: "But certainly God preserved the Jews and their religion through their centuries of diaspora as His chosen people."

Black castles: "For me the Jewish religion, like all other religions, is an incarnation of the most childish superstitions. And the Jewish people, to whom I gladly belong and with whose mentality I have a deep affinity, have no different quality for me.[10]

White: B-Q3: "Would you not agree that Jews have a distinctive place in the world?"

Black: P-KB4! "As far as my experience goes, they are no better than other human groups, although they are protected from the worst cancers by a lack of power. Otherwise, I cannot see anything 'chosen' about them."[11]

White: PxP *en passant*: "God is impenetrable, as the psalmist states. 'Many, O Lord my God, are thy wonderful works which thou have done, and thy thoughts which are toward us; they cannot be reckoned in order unto thee. If I would declare and speak unto them, they are more than can be numbered.'"[12]

Black: BxP! "Knowledge of the existence of something we cannot penetrate, of the manifestations of the profoundest reason and the most radiant beauty—it is this knowledge and this emotion that constitute the truly religious attitude; in this sense, and in this alone, I am a deeply religious man.[13]

"Ach, Max, if you castle, then I will move my knight to B3, and I will maintain material equality. Nor can you capture twice on your

K4 without losing a piece. Apparently, our position on the chess-board is even.[14] Let's continue the game tomorrow, perhaps without discussion of religion."

Max checked the front of the store to make sure there weren't any customers lingering. The coast was clear, and his formidable opponent, Albert Einstein, departed for the Institute.

REFERENCES

1. Einstein, A. (1931, March 29). "As Einstein sees America, " New York Herald Tribune (defunct) Magazine.
2. Reinfeld, F. (1959). *The complete chess course.* Doubleday and Company, p. 519.
3. Genesis 1,1, *Hebrew/ English Torah: The five books of Moses* (2012, p. 1). Varda Books.
4. Einstein, A. (2000). *The expanded quotable Einstein* (p. 202). Princeton University Press.
5. Einstein, A. 2000, p. 1.
6. Dukas, H., & Hoffman, B. (1954). Albert *Einstein, The human side: Glimpses from his archives.* Princeton University Press.
7. Albert Einstein, personal communication to Hoffman and Dukas, 1946.
8. Albert Einstein, personal communication to Professor Eric Gutkind, January 3,1954.
9. Albert Einstein, January 3, 1954
10. Albert Einstein, January 3, 1954
11. Albert Einstein, January 3, 1954
12. Psalm 40:5, *The book of psalms: In the authorized version* (1986, p. 65). Henry Holt & Co.
13. Einstein, A. (1956). *The world as I see it.* Citadel Press.
14. Einstein, A. (1956).

Author's Note: The lives of Albert Einstein and Max Lerner inter-sected in the early 1950s. Einstein played chess with Max Lerner in the back room of Max's Princeton stationery store, although whether or not they played the Vienna Game or had a conversation about religion, or the existence of God is uncertain. These are solely the creation of the author for this piece. Einstein's statements are from his public record and letters.

FIFTEEN

JUSTICE WITHOUT MERCY: RESENTMENT AND THE POLITICS OF EQUITY

The gilded sheath of pity conceals the dagger of envy.
—Friedrich Nietzsche

Cries for justice pervade the planet. If not for justice, then the appearance of justice. Whether for impoverished farmers, disadvantaged urbanites, or the declining middle class, strident demands to right the perceived wrongs of the past and present are widespread. These demands prescribe a progressive march forward to a future of equity. It is not the purpose of this essay to question such plaints, for it's no picnic to be poor or disenfranchised or hollowed out. Rather, let's analyze the motivation for parity from a philosophical perspective. Federal and state governments, public corporations, and educational institutions are falling all over one another to achieve some level of equity. Whether or not they are successful in these endeavors will depend on the philosophical motivation for such recompence.

Justifications proliferate for improving the conditions of the poor, enfranchising the marginalized, and restoring the middle class. These reasons include a call for fairness of opportunity, empathy for the downtrodden, and adherence to the ethics of the social contract. From the perspective of those who feel themselves wronged and their supporters who call for recompense, these motives are front and center in their demands for equity. The destitute need to be made whole, the aggrieved compensated, and a living wage imposed to preserve the middle class. However, the resentment or hostility of the wronged is rarely mentioned as the motive for recompense. Søren Kierkegaard (1813–1855), called this emotion *ressentiment* but did little to develop the idea. It fell on Friedrich Nietzsche (1844–1900) to advance the notion. So, what is ressentiment, and what role can it play in advancing social justice?

Among Nietzsche's works, *On the Genealogy of Morals* contains one of his most disturbing ideas about morality—namely, that its values stem from ressentiment of the oppressed (slaves). Nobility, valor, and arete are redefined by the exploited as evils and associated with arrogance, assertiveness, and avariciousness. Good embodies the opposite of these qualities. Therefore, a good man is one who least resembles the strong man.

> The problem with the other origin of the "good," of the good man, as the person of *ressentiment* has thought it out for himself, demands some conclusion. It is not surprising that the lambs should bear a grudge against the great birds of prey, but that is no reason for blaming the great birds of prey for taking the little lambs. And when the lambs say among themselves, "These birds of prey are evil, and he who least resembles a bird of prey, who is rather its opposite, a lamb,—should he not be good?" then there is nothing to carp with in this ide-

al›s establishment, though the birds of prey may regard it a little mockingly, and maybe say to themselves, "We bear no grudge against them, these good lambs, we even love them: nothing is tastier than a tender lamb.[1]

Goodness therefore lies in humility, meekness, and generosity. The noble Achilles of antiquity is told that "to be strong one is free to be weak." To be good, one is not exalted but humble, self-effacing, and without privilege. Christ's Beatitudes replaced Homer's heroic virtues. Christ taught them, saying,

> How blissful the destitute, abject in spirit, for theirs is the Kingdom of the heavens; How blissful those who mourn, for they shall be aided; How blissful the gentle, for they shall inherit the earth; How blissful for those who hunger for what is right, for they shall feast; How blissful the merciful, for they shall receive mercy; How blissful the pure in heart for they shall see God; How blissful the peacemakers, for they shall be called sons of God; How blissful those who have been persecuted for the sake of what is right, for theirs is the Kingdom of the heavens; How blissful you when they reproach you, and persecute you and falsely accuse you of every evil for my sake.[2]

The strong went along with the redefinition of virtue. After all, a predator in sheep's clothing also fares well among the weak.

Nietzsche neglects to provide an apposite definition of ressentiment or even to offer a translation into German. Nonetheless Max Scheler (1874–1928), a ressentiment authority, steps forward and draws out a definition that should suffice for the interests of this paper.

> Ressentiment is a self-poisoning of the mind which has quite definite causes and consequences. It is a lasting mental

attitude, caused by the systematic repression of certain emotions and affects which, as such, are normal components of human nature. Their repression leads to the constant tendency to indulge in certain kinds of value delusions and corresponding value judgments. The emotions and affects primarily concerned are revenge, malice, envy, the impulse to detract and spite.[3]

Does a self-poisoned mind lead to value delusions and value judgments that are based on vengeance, malevolence, and jealousy? If so, what form might such ressentiment take? "The head of the beast can only be cut off at one place; that's downtown Manhattan," roared filmmaker and activist Michael Moore (1954–), and the tender lambs marched to Wall Street.[4]

Occupy Wall Street, a generational watershed event, transmuted the idea of social justice into a broad movement that, in turn, transformed society in many ways. The protest's origins lay in the prior collapse of the mortgage market, resulting in massive unemployment and the near ruin of the world economy. Unemployed youth were angered by what they saw as corporate greed and the failure of capitalism as responsible for their situation. In 2011, scores of out-of-work millennials, many of whom were professionals, invaded Zuccotti Park in lower Manhattan and set up a tent community in protest of the expansive sense of inequality experienced by many Americans.

The rallying cry for these passionate activists became "we are the 99%," indicating the quantity of wealth held by the elite of the city compared to the masses while also commenting on the sheer size of the movement in comparison to the elites.[5] But with Occupy Wall Street, it wasn't necessary to convince the majority of Americans that greed rules Wall Street, that the banks have no one's interests but their own at heart, or that corporate America is out to squeeze every last bit of labor and wages out of everyone's pocket."[6] The Occupy Wall Street protest ended after two months when the tent city was cleared by the police as ordered by the mayor, but its effects nation-wide were profound.

The message of Occupy Wall Street spread far beyond Zuccotti Park, and a perfect storm of grievances was unleashed. In the minds of many, the excessive wealth of the few drained the small holdings of the masses. Corporate leaders were no longer the dynamos of the economy but purveyors of greed. The pervasiveness of intersection-ality revealed how different kinds of oppression—like those based on gender and race—intersected with one another. Racism denied opportunity for blacks and fostered police brutality and murder. The collapse of mortgages made the tent cities home for many. Capital-ists proliferated joblessness rather than new industry. College debt denied opportunity and constrained prospects for success. Soulless CEOs transferred jobs out of the country, leaving massive joblessness in their wake. Resentment, anger, and disgust followed the Occupy Wall Street protest from coast to coast and led to a call for justice without mercy.

There were many proposals for more parity and equitable wealth distribution. Tax the 1% to the hilt and reallocate funds to the 99%. Establish confiscatory estate taxes and a program of redistribution to equalize the wealth of the have-nots. Enact legislation for reparations for the descendants of slaves to penalize the former slave-holding society. Peel off all traces of slavery from the public square and strip the names of racists and slave holders from public and private spaces. Defund and penalize the police in reprisal for the perceived and real abuse of minorities. Absolve the mortgages of the hardworking as well as the profligate. Create a living wage for those who work and those who do not. Forget college debt and establish free universities for all. Force employers to bring companies back to the United States.

Such prescriptions for social justice may appear extreme to some as ressentiment calls for restoring the sense of equality that is a right for citizens and non-citizens. The problem with ressentiment, as with all negative intentions, is that it turns its malice back on its source, and as a result, the calls for justice result in injustice. Confiscate the wealth of the wealthy, and the result is poverty for all. Defund the police, and crime becomes rampant. Impose reparations for century-old slavery, and racism becomes structural racism. Compel corporations to insolvency, and joblessness becomes a depression. Sliver a culture from its history, and its legacy becomes hollow. Is the search for social justice a delusion rooted in ressentiment? In Plato's Republic we find that "the last extreme of injustice is to appear to be just without being so."

Much as we look to the day when cries for justice are satisfied or are replaced with social harmony, that day will not arrive if the malice of ressentiment is the philosophical basis of social change.

REFERENCES

1. Nietzsche, Friederich (1998). *On the genealogy of morality* (translated, with notes by Maudemarie Clark and Alan J. Swenson; Introduction by Maudemarie). Hackett Publishing Company.
2. Hart, David Bentley (2017). *The New Testament, A translation.* Yale University Press.
3. Scheler, Max (1972). *Ressentiment* (translated by William M. Holdheim; Introduction by Lewis A. Coser. Schocken.
4. Moore, Michael (2012, April). "The purpose of Occupy Wall Street is to occupy Wall Street," *Nation* 294 (14), 12.
5. Occupy Wall Street: "We are the 99%," blog posted 10/28/2019. https: overdrive.com/m
6. Moore, Michael (2012, April).

SIXTEEN

RED PORSCHE

Nobuddy ever forgets where he buried the hatchet.
—Kin Hubbard

On the way to my early morning freshman Ethics and Morals class, I encountered envy. It stood alone in a faculty parking spot, gleaming in the sun—a 1955 Porsche Sportster. The open-top convertible, the reddest of red, blazed as I approached it. Red piping highlighted the contours of the cream-colored bucket seats. A pair of leather driving gloves was draped casually on the meticulously designed dashboard. Inexplicably, a small fire extinguisher was strapped behind the seats, and a battered book-filled briefcase further marred the pristine interior.

I envisioned the powerful twin-carburetor rear engine that screamed high-speed racing, motoring with a girlfriend on the open road, or pulling up to a beach for an afternoon swim—everything a testosterone-laden seventeen-year-old desired. I thought of the owner, a professor, and at that moment I wanted what he possessed—and knew what I wanted to become.

I headed for class. We were to discuss envy from the text of the *Summa Theologica*. Borrowing from Aristotle, Thomas Aquinas

RED PORSCHE IMAGE © PETER KUMAR,
GULLWING MOTOR CARS, ASTORIA, NEW YORK.

defined envy as sorrow or sadness over another's good, because that good is regarded as something withheld or taken away from the envious person's excellence or reputation.[1] The instructor painted envy as a sin among the six other cardinal sins of Christian faith in that it stands in opposition to the virtue of charity. Envy becomes mortal when it is committed with full knowledge and full consent.

As a spiritual disorder, envy is the source of other sins, advised instructor, Dr. Eleanor, "Envy arouses an upward social comparison, a discrepancy between the envied and the envier. Often friends, siblings, coworkers are in a close personal relationship such that the discrepancy between have and have-not can be sharply painful. The comparative nature of envy is revealed when the envier denies what the situation is in comparison to what he or she desires it to be. The more someone thinks, '*it could have been me*' when someone else is better off, the more envious they become. Clearly envy comprises social comparison, but also evokes the emotions.[2]

Professor Eleonore continued: "Largely a negative emotion that commands body, mind, and action in response to a perceived threat

174

to the individual's self-view or personal goals caused by someone else being better off, envy energizes the envier to action to reduce the threat to his or her self-view by obtaining what the other has or by wishing that the other person loses the advantage. Both help the envier to deal with the threat by taking down the other's advantage or improving his or her self-regard."[3]

A student, Serena, raised her hand and asked, "Are all forms of envy malevolent or wicked? Sometimes I see my girlfriend Imelda wearing a beautiful pair of shoes that I would love to have, but with no thought that it is something that I am deprived of. Moreover, if Imelda does better than me on an exam, I may feel envious over her good fortune but do not feel that something was taken away from me."

"Some scholars point to a distinction between two types of envy: a malicious or invidious form and a benign, emulative, or admiring variety of envy,"[4] responded the instructor. "How do we define the cases in which envy is benign and separate them from cases in which it is not? In Aquinas's terms, the malicious envier desires that the rival lose the good, whereas the benign envier does not. But other philosophers claim that perhaps benign envy is not envy at all. This disagreement may boil down to a verbal dispute, but there seems to be a phenomenon that requires analysis. Can you think of examples of the proposed distinction that may obscure or clarify the issue?"

Argued Phil, "Professor, would you agree that not every case in which someone would like something that someone else possesses is a case of envy, as Serena suggested? Genuine envy involves sorrow or pain as Aquinas avers. Even to painfully desire someone's shoes is not to envy. So, every such desire should not be counted as benign envy. Maybe we are talking about longing rather than envy," he said.

"Thomas Young[5] suggests that what differentiates malicious envy and benign envy from mere longing is that in envy the subject is pained *because* the rival has the good," said Professor. "The reason or motivation for being in pain needs to be considered in envy. Perhaps the subject is bothered specifically by the difference in possession, not just by his own lack of the good.[7] But if this were so, how does it explain benign envy?"

"My neighbor Warren has so much more money than me; he is very rich. The disparity between my own impoverished assets and Warren's is really a bad thing. How could I not want Warren to lose some of his fortune to reduce the discrepancy? Even if none of the money he lost went to me, that would be preferable to the status quo. We see this idea of reducing wealth disparity in proposals to tax the rich. It matters not that the benefits trickle down to the public. It is the discrepancy of wealth that sticks in the throat of my generation. We are speaking of justice, Not envy," cried Leonid.

"Interesting digression, Leonid. "You made your point," replied Professor Eleonore. "Let's look at the work of Sara Protasi, who offers a more complex taxonomy of envy that includes a variety she calls 'emulative envy.'[6] She draws a matrix with two cross-cutting distinctions: whether the envier is focused on the rival or on the good and whether the envier perceives the good as obtainable or unobtainable. For Protasi, emulative envy falls within the quadrant that encompasses focus on the good that is obtainable. The envier feels that she can obtain the good without bringing down her rival while harboring her envy in an emulative form."

Questioned Judith, "If emulative envy is really a form of envy in which the envier cares only about the good and obtaining it and not perceived inferiority, then what role does being disadvantaged play? If inferiority plays no role, then why think of it as envy rather than some other emotion, perhaps admiration or longing?"

"Good observation," agreed Professor Eleanor "If emulative envy does include some worry about perceived inferiority distinct from the desire for the good, then how is this concern compatible with the insistence that there is no desire that the rival lose the good?[7] Perhaps emulative envy is not really envy at all. The missing key elements of a definition of envy are distress or sadness over another's good and taking down the rival. If a case cannot be made for emulative envy as a subcategory of envy, then perhaps it cannot be made for benign envy," suggested the professor.

At this point in the dialogue, I slipped into a reverie about the red Porsche. Was my experience a case of envy or one of longing? I thought of my own life situation as an undergraduate without much of an education, status, or assets in contrast to the owner of the car—a highly educated, highly regarded professor with wealth enough to purchase an expensive sports car. The disparity of our circumstances enflamed me, and the desire to have what he had gripped my being to the core. Could I complete my studies, achieve a doctorate and university position, engage and defeat the professor in debate? With a tenured professorship, I would have a lifetime job with money enough for expensive cars. I was scorched with envy.

The class ended with me lost in a heated dream state. Professor Eleanor left the room on her way to the red Porsche in the parking lot. I watched, transfixed, as she removed the straps from the fire extinguisher and turned its contents on me, warning,

Thou Shall Not Covet!

REFERENCES

1. Glenn, P.J. (2015). *A Tour of the summa.* Aeterna Press; ©1960 by B. Herder Book Co., St. Louis.
2. Van de Ven, N. (2016). Envy and its consequences: Why it is useful to distinguish between benign and malicious envy, *Social and Personality Psychology Compass, 106,* 337–349. doi: 10.1111/spc3.12253
3. Van de Ven, N. (2016).

4. Sterling, C., van de Ven, N., & Smith, R. (2016). *The two faces of envy: Studying benign and malicious envy in the workplace*. Oxford Online. doi:10.1093/acprof: oso/9780190228057.001.0001

5. Young, R. (1987). Egalitarianism and envy, *Philosophical Studies*, 52: 261–276.

6. Protasi, S. (2016). Varieties of envy, *Philosophical Psychology*, 29(4): 535–549. doi: 10.1080/09515089.2015.1115475

7. Protasi, S. (2016).

SEVENTEEN

BEING TOWARD DEATH: DAESIN AND DESCENDANTS

*Every parting gives a foretaste of death; every remeeting
a foretaste of the resurrection.*
—Arthur Schopenhauer

God may or may not be dead, but our being lives on through our descendants. While existentialism has wreaked havoc on the spiritual underpinnings of religion, a person's being persists through care of those he has touched and those who have touched him. So inquires Martin Heidegger, (1889–1976), whose moral compass took him to totalitarian depths but who, nonetheless, has something significant to say about the human condition as it faces death.

Heidegger opens his magisterial opus, *Being and Time*, indicating as inadequate Aristotle's (384-322 BC) definition of being: "whatever is anything whatsoever," spread over all 10 Aristotelian categories. Heidegger called for the necessity of explicitly restating the question of being, regarding it as inadequate because of the widely held belief that being's roots in ancient ontology makes its study unnecessary and superfluous and that, as a philosophical concept, being is supremely universal to the point of vacuity, resists definition, and is obviously self-evident. After all, everyone knows what being is, so its interpretation is without merit. Heidegger disagrees with this antiquated bias and calls for a uniquely human essence of being.[1]

By considering these prejudices, however, we have made plain not only that the question of being lacks an answer, but that the question itself is obscure and without direction. So, if it is to be revived, this means that we must first work out an adequate way of formulating it (*Being and Time*, p.24).

The idea behind *Being and Time* is straightforward: being is time and time is finite. Time ends with death. So, if one is to have an authentic life, one needs to confront one's death honestly. We need to project our life on the timeline of our death. Being-toward-death is the conception that brings the individual face to face with his mortality and the meaning of life.[2]

Daesin (being there) is Heidegger's term for being. It refers to the distinctively human experience that confronts such issues as selfhood, living with others while being alone with oneself and the inevitability of death. Daesin, being there, concerns involvement in the world. The world itself consists of relationships among entities, humans, and things, and such relationships end with death.

Heidegger's conception of being-towards-death severs relations toward the deaths of others; death is certain, indeterminate, and, in the final analysis, death trumps all. Death cuts off relations with kin or others. Death cannot be experienced through the death of others but only through my relation to my death. Death is certain, but we don't know when we will die. Finally, death outdoes all. It's the ultimate end; it "outstrips all the possibilities that my power of free projection possesses. Death is that limit against which my potentiality for being is to be measured. It is that essential impotence against which the potency of my freedom shatters itself.[3]

Robert Pirsig, (1928 -2017) who authored, *Zen and the Art of Motorcycle Maintenance,* was living in Sweden when word came that his son Chris was murdered in a mugging on the streets of San Francisco. Years before, father and son had motorcycled across the U.S. in Pirsig's philosophical quest for the metaphysics of quality, which was the narrative for the Zen book. Pirsig noted that while he and Chris lived apart for years and had relatively little contact, they were close. He asked, *Where did Chris go? He had bought an airline ticket that morning. He had a bank account, drawers full of clothes and shelves full of books. He was a real, live person, occupying time and space on this planet, and now suddenly where was he gone to? Did he go up the smokestack at the crematorium? Was he in the little box of bones they handed back? Was he strumming a harp of gold on some overhead cloud? None of these answers made any sense.*[4]

Pirsig went to Chris's room and touched his son's clothing and books in an attempt to rekindle his son's presence. Chris was an individual with a life, travel plans, a *daesin*, with concerns of selfhood, being with others, being alone. And all that remained were his ashes in a container. *The Chris I missed so badly was not an object but a pattern and although the pattern included the flesh and blood of Chris, that was not all there was to it. The pattern was larger than Chris and myself and related us in ways that neither of us understood completely and neither of us was in control of.*[5]

If anything, Pirsig's account describes a loving relationship between parent and child. Their lives were separate yet intertwined. "Death does indeed reveal itself as a loss, but a loss such as is experienced by those who remain. In suffering this loss, however, we have no way of access to the loss-of-Being as such which the dying man 'suffers.'" In Heidegger's words, the dying of others is not something which we experience in a genuine sense; at most we are always just "there alongside" (*Being and Time*, p. 282). Is this true? Are we merely a collateral presence in the death of one's child?

A child's death tears a huge hole in the center of all that. And the people who loved the child become desperate to fill that hole. They long for someone who can become a new object of love. They long for someone who can once again become the center of their caregiving patterns. Metaphorically speaking, we can describe that hole in center of the pattern as the "spirit" of the dead child. It is something invisible and real that remains behind and waits for a new body to enter.[6]

The death of a child is experienced fully as genuine. Heidegger's conception that "the only authentic death is one's own is both false and morally pernicious."[7] Most parents would trade their own lives for the survival of their child. While we may have no way of accessing the loss of being that Chris suffered when he was dying, nonetheless in the pain of his death, his parent suffered as if it were his own death. Death closes the possibility of continuing one's being into the future. We seek closure to fill the hole that the death of a child leaves.

Shortly after Chris's death, Pirsig's second wife, Wendy, became pregnant and gave birth.[8] *This time he's a little girl named Nell, and our life is back in perspective again. The hole in the pattern is being mended. A thousand memories of Chris will always be at hand, of course, but not a destructive clinging to some material entity that can never be here again. It was the larger pattern of Chris, making itself known at last.*[9]

The idea that the being of a deceased loved one lives in the memory of those left behind is both genuine and true. At times their being is transferred to another living being. In Pirsig's experience, Chris's being lives in his stepsister Nell. A healing of Chris's loss occurs and his material presence in memory is set free. We know not who or what orders such a transfer of love from one being to another. Perhaps God is not dead after all.

REFERENCES

1. Heidegger, M. (1962). *Being and time* (John Macquaire and Edward Robinson, trans.). Blackwell.
2. Critchley, S. (2009). Being and time, Part 6. *The Guardian.*
3. Critchley, S. (2009).
4. Pirsig, R. (1984, March 4). Looking ahead at the past. *New York Times Review of Books.*
5. Pirsig, R. (1984, March 4).
6. Pirsig, R. (1984, March 4).
7. Critchley, A. (2009).
8. Toft, D. (2018, August 4). Robert Pirsig on coming to terms with the death of his son.
9. Pirsig (1984, March).

EIGHTEEN

ADVERTISEMENTS FOR MY SELFIE

The Message is the Medium
—Anonymous

Are young people suffering from social media addiction (SMA)? Or are such behaviors a touch of youthful narcissism without adverse effects—but perhaps with profound consequences to world order? Clinicians claim that social media overuse is addictive behavior similar to gambling addiction, with severe mental health implications. According to psychiatrist Federica Pinna, revisions to the Diagnostic and Statistical Manual (DSM-5) extend addiction, customarily applied to psychotropic substances, to gambling as a "behavioral addiction" (BA).[1] The focus of the addiction is characterized by compulsive and uncontrollable gambling behavior. Does excessive social media use fall into this classification, or are the experts pathologizing ordinary behavior?

Norwegian psychologist Cecilie Andraessen and colleagues developed a scale to measure social media addiction. The Bergen Facebook Addiction Scale (BFAS) contains six core elements of addiction:

salience (dominates thinking and behavior), mood modification, tolerance, withdrawal, conflict, and relapse. It was administered to 423 participants, rechecked for reliability, and compared to other self-report scales for validity.[2] In a later national study with 23,500 participants' BFAS responses were correlated with responses on personality tests and self-esteem scales. Social media addiction (i.e., high BFAS scores) accounted for 17.5% of the variance and correlated with being young, female, and single. High BFAS scores also were related to higher narcissism and lower self-esteem scores.[3] The results suggest that the use of social media may serve to feed the ego and inhibit self-criticism.

Clinical psychologist Kimberly Young, director of the Center for Internet Addiction Recovery, developed the Internet Addiction Test (IAT) to measure the severity of online addiction and compulsive behavior, self-reported by adult users. The DSM-5 criteria for pathological gambling were applied to the unstandardized IAT for diagnosis of SMA. Dr. Young cautions against strictly measuring addiction to technology in terms of time spent but by how disordered someone's life has become because of it. Young declares that social media addiction is similar to drug and alcohol addiction, and recent research shows digital devices can affect the brain the same way that cocaine and heroin do.[4]

While some may suffer from SMA, what motivates the majority of social media consumers to sign on? Boredom, loneliness, and stress are cited as triggers for going online or texting. An action such as logging on to Facebook embodies variable rewards from scrolling through a mixture of juicy tidbits, liking someone's status updates, or posting a selfie and receiving positive feedback. Social media chitchat is rooted in self-disclosure, private experiences, and personal aspirations.

Young single women represent the vast majority of social media users who communicate (81 minutes daily) about themselves with others. Young men are also rabid users (60 minutes daily), but they spend more time on video games or watching movies than in chatting. Some 30 to 40 percent of daily conversations between individuals involve conversations about personal experiences, but up to 80 percent of postings are self-disclosures elicited by the language areas of the brain.[5] How does the propensity for self-disclosure affect the brain?

Research psychologists Diana Tamir and Jason Mitchell conducted a series of experiments that showed people derive intrinsic value from communicating information about themselves to others. Study participants were hooked up to an MRI (magnetic resonance imaging) unit and given the choice of talking about themselves, listening to others, or judging the ideas of others. Self-disclosure was strongly associated with increased activation of the brain's pleasure centers (mesolimbic dopamine system, including the nucleus accumbens and ventral tegmental area).[6] The increased activation of the limbic pleasure system was greater when the participants knew there was an audience and less when listening to or judging the comments of others. Furthermore, when money was offered as an alternative to self-disclosure, the participants chose talking about themselves.

Certainly, clinicians do not take issue with ordinary conversations or even habitual use of social media. A study of frequent cell phone use found that excessive use was related to fear of missing out (FOMO) on interesting tidbits and contacts, rather than addiction. An analysis of the IAT revealed six factors—salience, excessive use, neglecting work, anticipation, lack of control, and neglecting social life—as the norms for diagnosing SMA. Widyanto and McMurran replicated and extended Young's IAT survey and found evidence of neglecting work and social life among some users but little evidence of addiction.[7] A consensus is growing that the extent of SMA in the youth population may have been overstated.

A recent review of the scientific literature by Kuss and Griffiths concluded that social media attracted many habitual users but genuine addiction afflicted only a small minority of individuals.[8] A large-scale representative sample of 120,500 English adolescents was studied to determine the links between digital screen time and mental health.[9] Overall, there was very little evidence that "moderate use of digital technology is intrinsically harmful," and it "may be advantageous in a connected world."

Apparently, the mere act of sharing experiences about oneself stimulates brain areas that also are activated during pleasurable activities such as eating and sex—perfectly normal behaviors. Far from pathology, social media channels encourage messages dealing with issues of personal concern and delight. This drive to broadcast ourselves may facilitate the formation of social bonds, enhance social influence, forge social alliances, and elicit social feedback about personal attributes and attitudes.[10] Perhaps regular social media interaction is an adaptive response to the demands of a complex social world. However, there may be more profound consequences from the matrix of human communication.

It's been 50 years since Canadian philosopher Marshall McLuhan's book proposed that "The Medium is the Massage," a masterful play on words that stimulated animated global discussion about the media and its relation to the human condition. For McLuhan it was not the content that the media conveys, but the "medium itself that shapes and controls the scale and form of human association and action,"[11] Often our attention is focused on the content for the information it provides, while the subtle, long-term changes that the medium itself imposes on culture and the way we live are neglected. For instance, consider how Facebook has reshaped the dimensions of human communication.

Prior to the advent of social media, communication about ourselves occurred face to face, via phone chats, or through letters and notes—message forms that are increasingly passé. With Facebook, advertisements for ourselves are anonymous, personal, instantaneous, permanent, erasable, poly-audience, singular, and deliverable throughout the planet to faceless viewers as well as to "friends." The medium has allowed us to boldly reveal our political preferences, religious beliefs, sexual attitudes, and even snapshots of our private parts. How we make friends, choose confidants, and select mates on social media has broadened the universe of potential partners and even changed the edifice of marriage.

Pre-Facebook, gay marriage was vociferously and unanimously censured by politicians. The U.S. Congress passed the Defense of Marriage Act (DOMA) in 1996, restricting marriage to heterosexual couples. The social media outcry against the act and the push for gay and lesbian marriage was immutable and viral. Gay and lesbian political action groups formed to challenge the act through social media. Within two decades, the Supreme Court reversed DOMA and gay marriage was legalized. Social media are subtly changing the structure and scale of friendship, mate selection, and affiliation. We transmit our ideas, ambitions, and ourselves both locally and throughout the globe.

Social media institutions like Facebook and Twitter promote a message about themselves through an amalgam of the aspirations, ideals, and hopes of their many youthful users for a kinder, closer, more humane world. They have merged the content of their users' messages to one another with their respective corporate identity. Facebook's mission statement expresses the wishes of its users for a better world: "Facebook's mission is to give people the power to build community and bring the world closer together." It is no longer a mere profitable public corporation offering an enhanced platform for communication, but a distributor of power to the powerless. Twitter's mission statement draws inspiration from the same book: "to give everyone the power to create and share ideas instantly without barriers." YouTube makes a case for a world of voices in harmony: "Our mission is to give everyone a voice and show them the world."

McLuhan made a case for the power of the medium to change the world while we busily attend to the message. Indeed, Facebook and Twitter have insinuated themselves into many aspects of world culture—including politics, commerce, human relations—and continue to do so. But there are concerns about the scope of their reach in our lives as well as the possible mental health effects. While Mc-Luhan spoke of the medium as the message, perhaps the message has been hijacked as the medium for Facebook and Twitter.

REFERENCES

1. Pinna, F., Dell'Osso, B., Di Nicola, M., Janiri, L., Altamurs, A.C., Carpiniello, B., Hollander, E. (2015), Journal *of Psychopathology, 21*: 380–389

2. Andreassen, C. S., Torscheim, T., Brungorg, G.S., Pallesen, S. (2012). Development of a Facebook addiction scale, *Psychological Reports, 110*(2): 501–517.

3. Andreassen, C.S., Pallesen, S., Griffiths, M.D. (2106). The relationship between addictive use of social media, narcissism, and self-esteem: Findings from a large national study, *Addiction Behavior, 64*(10):1016.

4. Young, K., (2009) Internet addiction: The emergence of a new clinical disorder, *CyberPsychology & Behavior, 1*(3).

5. Walker, L (2018) Study: Social media fires up brain's pleasure center, *Lifewire,* https//www.life.com/social-media-stimulates-brain-pleasure-centers-26655245/print

6. Tamir, D., Mitchell, J. (2012, May). Disclosing information about the self is intrinsically rewarding. *Proceedings of the National Academy of Sciences, 109*(21): 80838–43.

7. Widyanto, L., & McMurran, M. (2004, August). *CyberPsychology & Behavior.* http://doi.org/10.1089/cpb.2004.7.443.

8. Kuss, D.J., & Griffiths, M.D. (2017). Social networking sites and addiction: Ten lessons learned, *International Journal of Environmental Research and Public Health, 14*: 311.

9. Przybylski, A. K., Weinstein, N. (2017), A large-scale test of the Goldilocks Hypothesis: Quantifying the relations between

digital-screen use and the mental well-being among adolescents, *Psychological Science,* 956797616678438. 10.1177/09567976166784

10. Yau, J., Reich, S. (2018) Are the qualities of adolescents' offline friendships present in digital interactions? *Adolescent Research Review 3*(3): 339–359.

11. McLuhan, M. (1964) *Understanding media: The extensions of man.* New York: Mentor; reissued 1994, with an introduction by Lewis Lapham. Cambridge, MA: MIT Press.

NINETEEN

DEPOLARIZATION

Progress celebrates Pyrrhic victories over nature.
—Karl Kraus

The neuron, first identified by the brilliant neuroanatomist Santiago Ramon y Cajal over a century ago, is the basic nervous system unit for the reception, processing, and transmission of electrochemical information within the brain. Several billion neurons make up our brain and nervous system and are responsible for the communication of energy that conveys our awareness of the world. Each neuron is an individual cell among a population of neurons that form an interacting community of specialized and general functions.

When we speak of polarization in these days of conflict and controversy, the reference often is to the political polarization of liberal and conservative, black and white, very rich and very poor, red states and blue states, Marxists and capitalists.

In contrast to the turmoil of political polarization, the polarized neuron remains in a resting state. The thin membrane covering each neuron maintains a stasis of charged particles called ions, with the interior of the neuron negative in relation to the surface of the membrane. While the neuron is in a resting state, the negative interior is maintained by differences in the charged ions within and outside of the membrane. On the membrane surface, abundant sodium ions carry positive charges, and within the neuron abundant potassium ions carry positive charges.

Sodium and potassium are similar. Both carry positive charges, and both are salts. The differences lie in their structure and concentrations along the cell surface and interior, kept apart by the impermeable membrane when the neuron is at rest. When the cell is excited, the membrane becomes permeable, allowing for the flow of positive sodium ions within, making the interior temporarily positive before the release of positive potassium ions restores the membrane to its negative internal state—all within a millisecond. The depolarization is transmitted along the surface of the neuron as a wave; this, in essence, is the message, which involves the transmission of energy within the neuron. Depolarization is essential for the transmittal of information within the nerve cell, and for communication between neurons within the nervous system. Depolarization is also essential for productive communication within a society.

In some ways, political polarization bears similarity to neural polarization. Just as salt ions are separated by a membrane that is both impermeable and permeable, political opposites are separated by ideology that is both fixed and fluid. Just as both sodium and potassium are necessary for communication within the neuron, political opposites are necessary for stability and change within a society. A society dominated by a single ideology or persuasion—conservative or liberal—without opportunity for an exchange of political direction, is dysfunctional.

Conservative societies, like royal dynasties preserved through inheritance, tend to ossify and become resistant to change. As a consequence, their social institutions harden, with social classes rigidly fixed and social innovation absent. Violent revolutionary societies seeking change begin with a bloodbath of traditional elements and eventually feed on their own members in an orgy of purges and pogroms.

When a conservative society attempts modest change from within, it is often unsuccessful and followed by upheaval. In late 18th century France, Louis XVI took the fatal step (for the monarchy) of calling an assembly of representatives of the main French social classes to replenish the national treasury. The French Revolution followed, and the aristocrats were guillotined. Tzar Nickolas of Russia turned over the conduct of the war effort in 1917 to the Duma. Revolution followed, the Bolsheviks established themselves, and the royal family was assassinated. Violent change is inherent in revolutionary societies, but the revolution itself becomes the victim of its violence.

The membrane of civility and cooperation is under stress when a society is locked in frozen polarity. A polarized neuron is activated by the flow of ions in and out of the membrane when evoked to threshold by a strong stimulus. A polarized society is stimulated to cooperation when facing an existential threat. For instance, the United States was in the grip of an anti-war movement at the time Europe was in the grip of Hitler. When Japan sunk the U.S. Navy's capital warships, the United States immediately declared war, the polarization ended, and the ensuing cooperation on foreign affairs between the political parties lasted for half a century. Does it take a catastrophe to depolarize competing societal factions?

Individuals in society are like neurons in the population of brain cells. Citizens make up a country's community just as neurons make up a brain's community. The neurotransmitters in a brain differ in their charges, as individuals in a community differ in personality. Modern personality theory postulates that conservative individuals tend toward the conscientiousness trait, and such individuals are often organized, dependable, careful, and prefer stability. Liberal individuals tend toward the openness trait and often are imaginative, independent, curious, and prefer change.

In the 1880s, Cajal was the first to realize that neurons were discrete entities, conducting their impulses in one direction only down their axon and receiving information through dendrites on the cell body; most notably, he noted a gap between one cell and the next—the synapse. Communication between neurons takes place at the synapse, the junction between communicating neurons that receives inputs, some of which excite the receiving cell and some of which inhibit the receiving cell. The response of the receiving cell depends on the crowd sourcing of competing inputs that excite and others that inhibit. In the same manner, liberal members of a political conclave excite the assembly and call for action, while the conservative group calls for restraint and seeks to inhibit change. When the liberals are ascendent, the body politic acts, and change takes place, just as the receiving neuron is brought to threshold and excited. When the conservatives dominate, action is curbed in the same way the receiving neuron is hyperpolarized and inhibited from firing.

Can it be that the brain is a microcosm of the commonwealth, and excitation and inhibition are necessary for both the brain and society to function? Thanks to the groundbreaking work of Cajal, we understand that change and stability are necessary for society to thrive just as depolarization and hyperpolarization of receiving neurons are required for the brain to function.

Cajal shared the 1906 Nobel Prize in Physiology and Medicine with Camillo Golgi, a gifted pathologist who developed the black reaction that revealed the cell structure of neurons in the brain. Golgi believed that his own observations of stained nerve fibers could support the traditional "reticular theory," which claimed that the nervous system was a syncytial system composed of an intricate network and that the nerve impulse was spread along this diffuse network. Cajal disagreed with the traditional view, and a bitter enmity divided the scientists. Cajal was the main supporter of the revolutionary "neuron doctrine," which correctly interpreted the nervous system as composed of anatomically and functionally distinct cells rather than cells in cytoplasmic continuity. Cajal and Golgi accepted the Nobel Prize in uneasy disagreement over the structure and function of the nervous system.

Let us acknowledge the wisdom of the Nobel Committee in investing both Santiago Ramon y Cajal and Camillo Golgi with the prize for their outstanding contributions to our understanding of the anatomy and function of the nervous system. Polarization and depolarization are inherent in nature's scheme. Often scientists approach a hypothesis from different, sometimes contradictory, assumptions, which leads to controversy and polarization. However, open debate allows for the depolarization of fixed opinions, which makes both revolutionary change and conservative tradition necessary in a dynamic society.

TWENTY

MIND AT LARGE

Persistent prophesy is a familiar way of assuring the event.
—George Gissing

ascination with the paranormal is not limited to the laity of be-
lievers but also extends to the clergy of research scientists. The
botanist J.B. Rhine directed extra-sensory perception (ESP)
laboratory studies at Duke University and gave definition to parapsychology as the psychology of the paranormal or Psi. Physicists
Harold Puthoff and Russell Targ conducted remote-viewing (RV)
studies at Stanford Research Institute in the 1970s and 1980s, funded
by the U.S. Military to spy on the armament facilities of the Soviet
Union through mental imaging.[1] Government grants of over $25 mil-
lion supported SRI research for over two decades. Rhine's institute
continues to receive funding from several foundations.

Once such parapsychology lab methods were vetted under controlled conditions, the Duke and SRI research was discredited and
termed pseudoscience.[2] It appears that in some studies the paranormal subjects were inadvertently cued by the investigators. Paradoxically, both Rhine and Targ maintained their conviction of the existence of the paranormal despite the negative evidence regarding their

research. To this day, Russell Targ writes and gives talks on the reality of the paranormal.

Perhaps clinging to a belief in the paranormal is not so absurd after all, whether by a scientist or you and me. Premonitions are common happenings over a large sample of individuals. Most of us or someone we know has had a premonition or a dream of an event that happened later just as it was experienced. Occasionally, some of us communicate remotely with another person distantly in time or space—perhaps a dream conversation with the departed or the awareness of an absent friend who relates through Psi an event soon to happen. The religious may experience contact with the Madonna, Moses, or Mohammed. Such powerful experiences are arresting and unforgettable. On the other hand, the many, many failed intuitions are forgotten. Are these psychic experiences a matter of chance, or can the mind wander?

Let's look at some of the qualities of consciousness, and whether it can travel–not that a catalogue of these features is by any means complete; consciousness has a complexity that defies analysis.[3] Consciousness is private; it integrates the senses, vision, hearing, and touch as a unified experience. Our awareness is not only of the world around us but also of the world within us.[4] We experience the products of consciousness—our thoughts, emotions, desires—not the process of consciousness; how we come to an idea, a feeling, or a wish is unavailable to us. William James[5] described consciousness as like a river—always moving, ever changing, sometimes cascading, sometimes still. Just as we cannot put our foot in the same part of the river twice, our conscious awareness fluctuates moment to moment. Does consciousness stay within us as a strictly a local presence, personal and whole, or can it separate from the body and travel?

Reports of near-death experiences (NDE) suggest out-of-body experience (OBE) in that twilight zone between life and death. OBE descriptions contain similar elements: falling or rising through a tunnel to a lighted being, hearing noises, sensing the presence of non-physical beings. Not all near-death experiences involve OBE. Psychiatrists Glenn Gabbard and Stuart Twemlow[6] studied several hundred reports of NDEs and found OBE, a separation of mind and body awareness in many cases. These authors differentiated OBEs from other altered states of consciousness, psychiatric disorders, meditation, and drug effects and consider them unique. Respondents describe the OBE experience as purposeful, beneficial, spiritual, and transformative. Gabbard and Twemlow claim that a paranormal explanation for OBE is the only one that agrees with the interpretation of the NDE descriptions—namely, that the soul separates from the body. The researchers surveyed NDE individuals outside of a laboratory setting. What happens when the paranormal is brought into the laboratory and studied under controlled conditions?

My thrilling experience in the late 1970s as a participant in a remote-viewing experiment at SRI was the culmination of a year-long fascination with Puthoff and Targ's paranormal research. Through correspondence with the researchers, I was invited to the laboratory to be a subject in a remote-viewing study. Like other subjects, I had occasional dreams and premonitions but no RV training. On arrival at the SRI lab, I was ushered into a sound-attenuated chamber roughly 6 by 6 by 8feet and given a simple RV lab task to test my paranormal abilities. I was instructed to relax, clear my mind of distractions and concerns, breathe deeply, and sit quietly in the chamber for about 15 minutes. A calm mind was required. My RV task was to locate a number on a clock-shaped screen with ten numbers that was outside of the chamber. For instance, if the number 5 was called in through the intercom, I was to make a mental imagine of it among the other numbers on the screen. Once a response was given, let's say, number 5 was at 6 o'clock, the numbers were scrambled, and again I was asked to remotely locate a number. This protocol involved some 20 trials; the testing ended, and I was released from the chamber.

"Well, how did I do?

My hosts smiled. "You missed every location."

"Oh, so I am not a remote viewer."

"True, but there was a curious result. When the number to be viewed was at 3 o'clock, you said 9 o'clock; when it was a 2 o'clock, you reported 8 o'clock. You had a run of such responses that were statistically significant beyond chance."

"You mean a kind of obverse remote viewing?"

"Indeed, it appears that way.'

"Looks like my mind wandered but lost its way."

In the years since J.B. Rhine undertook the scientific study of ESP, considerable strides have been made cataloguing paranormal phenomena and even validating OBEs under near-death conditions. At the heart of the paranormal, the conscious mind extends itself beyond the individual, beyond space, and even beyond time. Consciousness itself is that profound noetic mystery that resists our understanding yet is of us, with us, and beyond us.

REFERENCES

1. Tart, C. Puthoff. H. and Targ, R. (1979). *Mind at large: The Institute of Electrical, Electronic, Engineers Symposia on the nature of extra sensory perception.* Praeger.

2. Hines, T. (2003). *Pseudoscience and the paranormal.* Prometheus Press.

3. Hart, D. (2017). *The dream child's progress and other essays.* Angelico Press.

4. Eysenck, M. (2015). *Cognitive psychology: An introduction* (7th ed.). Psychology Press.

5. James, W. (1890). *Psychology* (Vol. I), American Science Series, Advanced Course. Henry Holt & Co.

6. Gabbard, G., &Twemlow, S. (1985). *With the eyes of the mind: Empirical analysis of out of body experiences.* Praeger Publishers.

TWENTY-ONE

NOT EVERY MAN CAN WEAR LEOPARD BRIEFS

No one hates his body.
—Saint Augustine

B each Scene: Teenage boy and girl on a blanket. A burly older man tears by.

"Hey, you're kicking sand in our face!" shouts the boy.

"Aw, shut up, you skinny runt!" The husky tough guy slaps boy, humiliating him in front of his girl, who sighs in distress.

Boy goes home upset, kicks a chair in fury, and decides to sign up for the Charles Atlas Dynamic Tension Body Building Program as advertised in a magazine.

Over 50 years, a confident Charles Atlas, in leopard print briefs, was famously pictured in ads appearing in boys' magazines of every stripe, from comic books, auto, model railroading, adventure tales, and scouting magazines, to Popular Science. His erect, bronzed, muscular, perfectly sculpted torso filled the page with a smiling invitation: "YOU CAN HAVE A BODY LIKE MINE!!"

An early Charles Atlas ad

Ad featuring an older Charles Atlas

The ad copy varied, but the same theme remained. A skinny young man is bullied and taunted in front of his girl, "Hey, you bag of bones, get lost!" At times he is punched, at other times slapped or knocked over. At home he resolves to reconfigure his body through the Charles Atlas program, which promised that "within a week you will see a change in your body."

The 12-step program consisted of a daily routine of obligatory chin-ups, sit-ups, and push-ups, along with a series of activities in which the muscles of the arms and legs were placed in tension for several minutes. Some exercises were isometric, others isotonic. No weights or equipment were required, and all the activities could be done at home. After a week of rigorous conditioning, the boy felt better about himself and was motivated to continue the program. With a persistent daily routine that faithfully followed Atlas's guide, some young men would show gains in muscle tone, strength, appetite, and weight.

In boyhood, President Theodore Roosevelt experienced being the "skinny runt." He was bullied and punched by a couple of older boys, who taunted and beat him. Like the boy in the Atlas advertisements, he undertook a program of physical exertion, developed a strong physique, and a lifelong love of vigorous activity. He adopted "the strenuous life," as he entitled his 1901 book, as his ideal, both as an outdoorsman and as a politician."[1]

What motivated Roosevelt to vigorous activity and young men to the Charles Atlas program was the desire for self-development. The appeal of self-help programs, whether for body building or winning friends and influencing people, is based on a perceived self-deficiency that preys on a young man's insecurity. The shortfall may be in physical strength or vigor, but more often it is related to a broad range of traits regarding what it means to be a man.

Charles Atlas proved to be a model of masculinity for millions of men.[2] Born Angelo Siciliano in Acri, southern Italy, he emigrated to New York with his family in 1903 when he was 10. As a teenager, he was the proverbial 97-pound weakling and experienced hazing at the beach while with a girl. Resolute in his desire to build himself up, he found traditional exercises like sit-ups and push-ups lacking in producing the desired results. At the Brooklyn Museum, sculptures of Hercules, Apollo, and Zeus inspired his conditioning goals. Watching lions in the Bronx Zoo as they actively stretched, contracted, and extended their muscles gave Angelo the idea of a unique conditioning program to increase muscle mass and strength. Gazing at a stretched-out lion, he asked himself: "Does this old gentleman have any barbells, any exercisers?. . . And it came over me. . . . He's been pitting one muscle against another."[3]

Within a few years, Angelo's perfectly formed body propelled him to a career as an artist's model; he posed for over 70 public statues including Rockefeller Center's. Later he changed his name to Charles Atlas and formed a company with advertising genius Charles Ronan. Together they organized a campaign for the Dynamic Tension Body Building 12-Step Program. The hazed and beaten boy unable to defend his girl at the beach was shown repeatedly as Charles Atlas called on his audience to build up their bodies and, by implication, their self-confidence and masculinity. The ads were ubiquitous in boys' and men's magazines for six decades and led to historic sales for a body-building program. Daily letters poured into the company from young men extolling the 12-step program and seeking counsel from Charles Atlas.[4]

"Live clean, think clean, and don't go to burlesque shows" was at the heart of the advice dispensed by Atlas in the 1930s and1940s. Atlas neither smoked nor drank and his life was scandal free. His exercises were framed with detailed lifestyle advice on how to dress, sleep, breathe, eat, and relax."[5] Atlas answered letters with a paternal touch, asking whether the young man attended church and how life was going for him. Implicit in his counsel was that while physical well-being was important, strength of character was preeminent. However, the Atlas message of masculinity is rooted in biology, as an analysis of the ubiquitous beach scene reveals.

The young man and his girl were on a blanket under an umbrella, suggesting domesticity. Partially naked and exposed, they had laid out a territory for building their relationship. The husky tough guy invaded this "household" by kicking sand on the couple, thereby asserting his interest in the girl. If the girl had not been present, the burly guy most likely would not have paid any attention to the boy, except perhaps to cast a disdainful glance or hurl an insult. The boy was beaten by the tough guy to establish male dominance in the presence of a female. Unable to defend himself and the girl, the vanquished boy retreated. The girl sighed with disappointment, leaving the boy feeling impotent, forlorn, and angry.

Animal groupings are organized in hierarchies entrenched in billions of years of evolution. This is true for all animal species, including humans.[6] A social hierarchy is pyramidal, with individuals arrayed from top to bottom in terms of dominance. The individual at the top of the hierarchy, a male, is often more aggressive or successful in beating down competitors to lower positions in the order. The dominant male attracts females and procreates more often. Individuals at the lower rungs fend for themselves for whatever sex partners are left over. Was the beach scene drama so remote from the theater that has played out over many centuries across all species?

Charles Atlas's promise in the cartoon ad brought a different ending to the story, an ending that defied evolution. The boy sent a check for $29.95 and obtained the 12-Step Dynamic Tension Body Building Program. He followed the steps of the program and transformed his body. On returning to the beach, he smashed the bully's face with. "Hey fella—no more pushing small guys around. I am a man and I stand my ground." How fitting that the girl comes up to him and adoringly gushes, "Oh Mac, you are a man after all," to the delight of the beach crowd. In the end, the guy gets the girl and society's adulation as a hero.

Not every man can wear leopard print briefs and get away with it. In fact, very few graduates of the 12-Step Dynamic Tension Program attained Charles Atlas's physique. yet many praised the results it wrought on their self-confidence. As with any difficult resolution to change one's behavior, most respondents dropped the exercises and returned to old habits. However, the implicit message Atlas conveyed strikes a chord with young men worldwide to this day.

A strong body in fitness and health is necessary to take charge of one's life. Beyond the beach scene stage, a world exists that is contentious, capricious, and chaotic. Strength of character and a clear purpose of being is required of a man to stand up to life's challenges. Body and mind must face adversity erect in duty, chest out in confidence, and head up in vision to conquer the chaos of life.[7] For men and boys, Charles Atlas's masculine message appealed to millions who found that there was more than having artist's model body to being a man.

REFERENCES

1. Roosevelt, T. (1901). *The strenuous life.* New York: Dover.
2. Gaines, C., & Butler, G. (1982). *Yours in perfect manhood: Charles Atlas: The most effective fitness program ever devised.* New York: Simon & Schuster.
3. Gaines, C., & Butler, G. (1982).
4. Black, J. (2009, August). "Charles Atlas: Muscle man," *Smithsonian Magazine*, p. 4.
5. Black, J. (2009).
6. Sapolsky, R. M. (2017). *Behave: The biology of humans at our best and worst.* New York: Penguin.
7. Petersen, J. (2018). *12 rules for life: An antidote to chaos.* Toronto: Random House Canada.

TWENTY-TWO

TO SLEEP, PERCHANCE TO DREAM

Among all human constructions, the only ones that avoid
the dissolving hands of time are castles in the air.
—Federico De Roberto

A t times, we encounter from our student days the name of an individual who was highly influential in our education. A scientist who enshrined our understanding of human behavior as a unified material reality. Such a happenstance recalls that profound influence in our youth but also may reveal that human constructions may be nothing more than dreams.

A recent obituary for William Dement (1928-2020), called The Father of Sleep Medicine, filled an entire page in the New York Times.[1] An early researcher of sleep, he was among the first to bring subjects into a sleep laboratory to slumber as brain activity (EEG), eye movements, heart rate, respiration, and body temperature were measured. He was also a cool guy who played bass at jazz clubs. As a medical intern in New York, he set-up a sleep laboratory in his apartment, and invited Rockette dancers to serve as research subjects in sleep deprivation studies.

Nathanial Kleitman's laboratory at the University of Chicago first sparked Dement's lifelong passion for sleep research and for understanding the relationship between rapid-eye movements and dreams. In his biography Dement proudly asserted, "I believe that the study of sleep became a true scientific field when I finally was able to make all-night continuous recording of the brain and eye activity during sleep."

Dement documented that the sleep cycle passed from drowsiness through several 90-minute cycles from light to deep sleep, which were interrupted saccadic eye movements. These rapid eye movements, or REM periods, were often accompanied by dream reports once the participant was awakened. All subjects reported dreaming several times in each sleep session.[2] Here, finally, was an exciting scientific method that appeared to provide a physiological record of what was occurring in the brain as a person was asleep and dreaming. The representation of the dream was captured in the subject's recall of it when awakened.

For some must watch while some must sleep.
So runs the world away.
—Hamlet

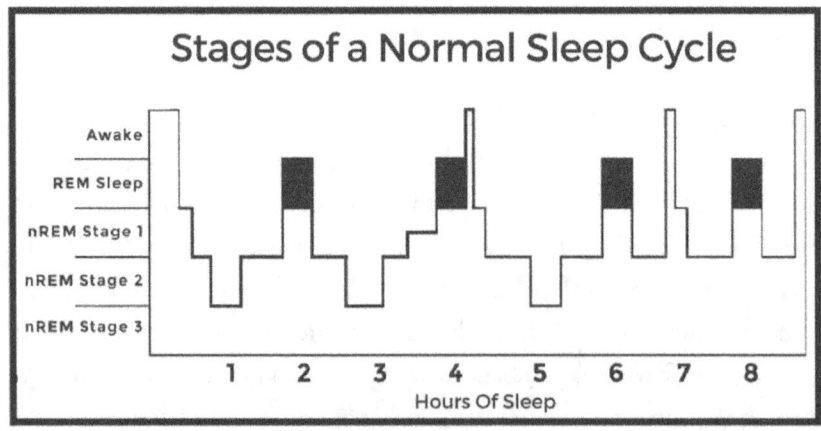

Dement's research fostered the idea, now prevalent among neuroscientists, that the brain activity was the material basis of conscious experience and, further, that unconscious processes like dreaming could be fully understood as reflections of brain function. Researchers Alan Hobson and Robert McCarley suggested that dreams are the result brain activity caused by the spontaneous firing of specific neurons in the brain stem during REM, which triggers random neural activity in the visual system and cerebral cortex. The cortex struggles to synthesize and make sense of the random activity with the creation of a dream.[3] Hobson and McCarley proposed that even though the source of dreams is random, the dreamer's daytime motivations, experiences, and memories may guide the interpretation of dream content.

With such thrilling advances in neuroscience on the physiology of sleep and dreaming, were not the mysteries of the mind itself soon to be uncovered? Graduate students like myself entered our professional lives in high hopes that we would lead the way to a scientific understanding of consciousness. After all, powerful correlations were established between and among EEG activity, rapid eye movements, and the dream state. Were there not other aspects of human behavior to understand as reflections of underlying physiology?

A few years later, William Masters and Virginia Johnson employed physiological measures to uncover the human sexual response cycle as couples copulated in their laboratory. Participants were hooked up to devices that measured brain wave activity, heart rate, respiration, body temperature, and sexual tumescence. Masters and Johnson used prostitutes to serve as participants in their research because they felt that female subjects would not be available (even though it was the 1960s, sex without love was considered distasteful). Like sleep, the human sexual response revealed a cycle consisting of several phases: excitement, plateau, orgasm, and resolution. Masters and Johnson published a book of their findings for scholars, which. broke sales records for a studious book on sex research.[4]

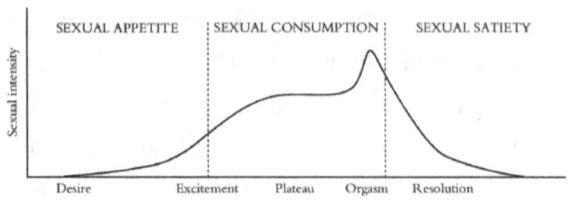

SEXUAL RESPONSE CYCLE

Dement and Masters showed that intimate private aspects of human behavior were subject to physiological recording that yielded fairly precise correlates of sleep and sex. This gave impetus to the idea that human behavior was nothing more than a material enterprise. It was assumed that future research would reduce consciousness itself to the neurochemistry of brain function. Our sexuality, dreams, and awareness were wholly part of the material world.

Kleitman disregarded the dream reports as a significant finding, but for Dement, who intended a career in psychiatry, the study of dreams was, as Freud said, *the royal road to the unconscious*. A dream is a life-like experience during sleep that is accepted as real by the dreamer. Dreams create a narrative of the dreamer's world. Do dreams have a purpose? Do dreams have meaning?

The distinction between the purpose or function of dreams and the meaning of dreams has concerned sleep scientists since the discovery of REM. However, for psychoanalysts the theater of the night created salient symbols that exposed the patient's unconscious thoughts, conflicts, and anxieties. Indeed, a dream had meaning that was revealed though interpretation when the patient was awake. As Dement and his colleagues framed the question of the meaning of dreams. The major technique by which psychoanalysts attempt to arrive at the hidden meaning of a dream is called free association. A patient will think about an image from a dream or a whole dream and without inhibition or censorship say whatever comes to mind. This usually occurs without difficulty and the thought usually seems important and clarifying. If the psychoanalyst has worked with the patient for a long time, he or she often knows where the ideas and associations are leading, or that they can relate to certain aspects of the patient's personality or life. The fact that the psychoanalyst knows the patient extremely well introduces an obvious bias to an interpretation.[5]

In large measure, the meaning a dream has for us is the meaning we confer upon it while we are awake. We may freely associate and report our recollection of the dream, not the dream experience. If the meaning of dreams depends on the wakened dreamer, then is the content meaningful while the dreamer is asleep? Sigmund Freud would certainly say yes—that the unconscious mind has the intention to reveal a conflict or desire to consciousness. Accordingly, the meaning of a dream is inseparable from the dreamer's state of awareness. The hidden meaning is transferred unchanged from unconscious to conscious states. Is this so? Most dreams are forgotten upon waking, or not even reflected upon as we go about our daily activities. Many dreams are a jumble of inchoate, fragmentary images and thus not open to interpretation. So, perhaps the significance placed on hidden meaning is overstated. Maybe dreams are fragments of consciousness without consequence. But do dreams have a purpose? Or, like hidden meaning, are they castles in the air?

Alan Hobson denied dreams of any function in sleep. He asserted that dreaming was a byproduct of REM sleep without purpose: "Because dreams are so difficult to remember, it seems unlikely that attention to their content could afford much in the way of high-priority survival value. Indeed, it might be assumed that dreaming is an epiphenomenon of REM sleep whose cognitive content is so ambiguous as to invite misleading or even erroneous interpretation"[6] In a later paper, Hobson suggested that prior daytime experiences and motivations may be integrated into the dream[7].

The early work of Dement and others hypothesized that rapid-eye-movement sleep was the neurophysiological substrate of dreaming. This triggered a cascade of research over the next six decades into the function or purpose of REM sleep. Memory consolidation, emotional regulation, threat simulation, and the individuation of personality were among the models suggested as functions of dreams. However, Dement's hypothesis was challenged because even after decades of research, it could not explain the characteristics of dream reports, let alone dreams themselves. "Therefore, even the neurophysiological correlates of dreaming are still unclear, and many questions remain unresolved. Do the representations that constitute the dream emerge randomly from the brain, or do they surface according to certain parameters? Is the organization of the dream's representations chaotic or is it determined by rules?"[8] These are significant questions that have eluded explanation; however, the essence of the hypothesis—the neurophysiological substrate of dreams—was ignored.

How do we reduce the dream experience, not merely the dream report, to brain activity? How do we move from the subjective experience to the material events in the brain? What is the material basis of dreams? The question was ignored for good reason. It is not possible to reduce conscious or unconscious experience to brain activity in any way.

Matter and mind are separate categories of reality. Natural philosopher Rene Descartes (1596–1650) ran into the same problem of mind and body as separate realities—soul and matter—that interacted through the brain's pineal gland. Material things like the brain were controlled by physical laws; immaterial things like consciousness were controlled by non-physical laws. What was the nature of the energy transfer between immaterial mind (soul) and the material body (brain)? Was the energy transfer material, or was the energy transfer spiritual? If either were true, then what was the nature of the interaction? In what way did spirit affect matter, and what of the reverse? This was the conundrum for students of mind and brain.

Neuroscientists blithely replied, "There is no problem, the soul does not exist! There is a single unified material reality." Dreams are emergent events that are integrated within the neurophysiology of the brain. But now we are back to the original question: If the neurophysiological substrate of dreams is objectively physical, how do we explain the subjective experience of the dream itself?

Ay there's the rub.

REFERENCES

1. New York Times (2020, June 30. William Dement obituary.
2. Dement, W., & Kleitman, N. (1957). The relation of eye movements during sleep to dream activity and body motility. *Journal of Experimental Psychology,* 53, 339–346.
3. Hobson, J. A., & McCarley, R.W. (1977). The brain as a dream-state generator: An activation-synthesis hypothesis of the dream process. *American Journal of Psychiatry,* 134, 1335–1348.
4. Masters, W., & Johnson, V., (1966). *Human sexual response.* Boston: Little Brown.
5. Pelayou, R., Dement, W., & Singh, K. (2017). *Dement's sleep and dreams.* Independent Paperback.
6. Hobson, J.A. (1998). *The dreaming brain.* New York: Basic Books.
7. Hobson, J. A. (2014). Lecture II Physiology. In N. Tranquillo (Ed.), Dream consciousness: Alan Hobson's new approach to brain and its mind (pp. −51). Cham: Springer.
8. Ruby, P.M. (2011, November). Experimental research on dreaming: State of the art and *neuropsychoanalytic* perspectives. *Frontiers of Psychology, 18.* https://doi.org/10.3389/fpsyg.2011.00286

TWENTY-THREE

THE TRANSCENDENTAL PYRAMID

The first forty years of life give us the text;
the next thirty supply the commentary.
—Arthur Schopenhauer

The quest for self-improvement is an enduring human motive, as attested by the legion of popular self-help books, courses, videos, and schemes that offer the consumer a way of unlocking the power of his or her true persona. The promise of finding the essence of self-improvement is the basis of such pursuits. Whether Dale Carnegie's *How to Win Friends and Influence People*, the classic self-help book, or Jordan Peterson's most engaging YouTube lectures on self-improvement, these products tap into a powerful desire to transcend one's prosaic existence. Perhaps there is potential within us that when actualized will reveal our "noble" self, which Jean Jacques Rousseau suggested was the true nature of humans.

THIRD FORCE

Psychologists rejoining the mechanistic postulates of behaviorism and negative determinism of psychoanalysis turned to humanism as a positive third force in the behavioral sciences. Abraham Maslow did not originate humanistic psychology but was very much present in formulating its principles. In childhood, Maslow saw himself as a shy, depressed, lonely, self-reflective neurotic. Impelled by these inadequacies, he majored in psychology in college and took his doctorate with the famous comparative psychologist Harry Harlow. As a university professor in pre-World War II days, Maslow found himself in the presence of eminences such as Alfred Adler, Ruth Benedict, Viktor Frankl, and Kurt Goldstein, whom he embraced in collegial friendship.

Other than Pavlov's dog in harness, no image is more palpable in psychology books than Maslow's Hierarchy of Needs pyramid. As a guide to explaining motivation, it is omnipresent in management, education, sociology, marketing, politics, and ethics textbooks and resources. The hierarchy of needs is both an icon of motivation and a representation of human development.

Drawing on his work with Harry Harlow on the sexuality and dominance in primates and his close friendships with psychoanalysts Alfred Adler and Kurt Goldstein, Maslow assembled a catalog of human motivation that had five tiers.[1] At the pyramid's base lies an instinctive inner core that serves the basic needs of hunger, thirst, contact comfort, and sex—needs that remain in the individual throughout the lifespan. Maslow was not a biological determinist, but he saw the base as composed of a kind of biological raw material. When this material is nurtured by the family and allowed to develop within a cultural environment that encourages the process of self-discovery, it can provide an organismic potential for growth.

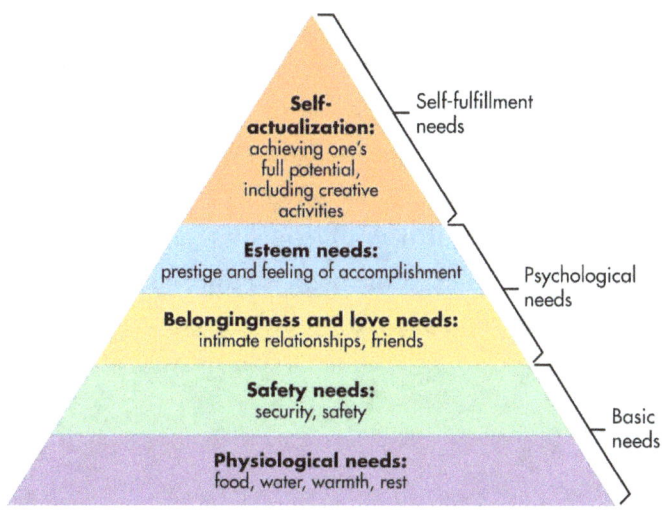

MASLOW'S HIERARCHY OF NEEDS

There follows a tier of safety and security needs that prompt the individual to seek pleasure and avoid pain. The next tier recognizes the need to belong, to give and receive love, to affiliate with others and gain their acceptance. This is followed by a tier of esteem needs to achieve, be competent, gain recognition, and excel. At the top of the pyramid is the transcendent need for self-actualization. Maslow[2] saw as the need for self-fulfillment and the realization of one's potential. But then, self-actualization became something more.

SELF-ACTUALIZERS

When he first proposed his hierarchy of needs, Maslow may have felt that the first four tiers covered the bulk of humanity's basic and psychological needs. After all, when survival, attachment, and esteem needs are met, what more could one want or require? In his initial formulations of the theory, Maslow felt that very few individuals actually achieve self-actualization.[3] Abraham Lincoln, Albert Einstein,

Mohandas Gandhi, and Eleanor Roosevelt came to mind, but few others. Based on his interviews and biographies of colleagues who had escaped from Nazi Germany, Maslow selected them, and included himself, as self-actualizers. Paradoxically, but understandably, it is unlikely that he considered Adolf Hitler a self-actualizer. Only saints need apply. A criticism of needs hierarchy theory is the small sample of self-actualizer elites in the theory. However, as the humanistic psychology movement expanded, so did the construction of self-actualization.

CONSTRUCTIONISM

Like the genetic epistemologist Jean Piaget, Maslow and the humanistic psychology leaders were constructionists. With an emphasis on learning, constructionists placed prominence on the environment rather than inborn nature in describing human knowledge. Knowledge is built, layer upon layer, on previous knowledge. People learn to learn, which involves constructing systems of meaning. Learning is an active process that encompasses the need to engage in the world. Moreover, learning is a social activity—contextual and personal. In Piaget's words, "The principal goal of education in the schools should be creating men and women who are capable of doing new things, not simply repeating what other generations have done; men and women who are creative, inventive and discoverers, who can be critical and verify, and not accept, everything they are offered."[4] In essence we construct our world; reality itself is a construction.

At the pinnacle of the hierarchy of needs, self-actualization stands as the high point of personal development. Self-actualizers desire to fully expand their potential and seek to satisfy a deep curiosity about life's meaning through a process of self- discovery and peak experiences. The transcendental need to experience cosmic mysteries through moments of intense bliss and intuitive comprehension is called "the oceanic experience." Late in his life, Maslow[5] expanded self-actualization to include cognitive and aesthetic needs and established transcendental psychology to further explore human development.

NEEDS DEMOCRATIZED

Gradually, the needs hierarchy theory (NHT) democratized and spread to cultural institutions such as commerce and education, as well as to the public in their quest to become the best version of themselves. Workplace applications of the NHT call for a clean, well-lighted workspace, with healthcare, dining facilities, and rest and recreational facilities. Safety of employees becomes a necessity; the Federal Government even created the Occupational Safety and Health Administration (OSHA) to ensure employee health and safety in the workplace. It is not always easy to for those in a large company to feel they belong. Organizations that value social contact among employees host social events so that employees get to know one another, in the expectation that increases in productivity will result. Esteem resulting from the recognition of work well done leads to advancement and increased responsibility.[6] A company can foster self-actualization by maximizing employees' potential for work and encouraging out-of-the-box creative solutions to work problems.

Applications of NHT in the classroom thrive throughout the spectrum of grade levels, from elementary school through college.[7] Federal programs provide free food to poor children so that basic nutrition standards for all pupils are met. The safety needs of children in and around the school are seen to by crossing guards, monitors, security staff, and school safety programs. If a child arrives at school with cuts or bruises, school personnel are required to report such instances to the authorities. Love and belonging needs are encouraged by the sensitive teacher, who arranges seating in question-and-answer dialogues so that the shy or withdrawn student has the opportunity to engage with others. For holidays, teachers request that each pupil send a greeting card to all the other children in the class. Esteem needs are met with sincere compliments for work well done—and even not so well done—and affirmation from teachers and peers. Are the students reaching their full potential and utilizing their strength to achieve self-actualization?

As is evident, most applications of the hierarchy model to the workplace and school settings are products for consumption of the feel-good culture that humanist psychologists and others have advanced. The applications are two-edged. Creating an overused employee rest and recreation center may lessen workplace motivation and diminish company performance. Social events among employees may result in inappropriate liaisons that damage company harmony. There is the risk that the self-actualizer will leave the firm and create a start-up in competition with the former employer. Criticisms of the research base of NHT in biographies and interviews have followed Maslow to the grave and continue to this day.

CRITICISM

The critiques take several forms: validity of the hierarchy, confinement of sexuality as a biological drive in the first tier, and neglect of collective societies.

In their extensive review of research on Maslow's theory, Wahba and Birdwell[8] found little evidence for the validity of Maslow's hierarchy. The authors stated: "Maslow's Need Hierarchy Theory has received little clear or consistent support from the available research findings. Some of Maslow's propositions have been totally rejected, while others have received mixed and questionable support at best."

The theory, in their view, is almost non testable" because clear operational definitions of each need construct are lacking, but mainly because it is difficult to measure the relative satisfaction of needs and the precise extent to which a need must be satisfied before the next need emerges, or even what a need is: Is it psychological and/or physiological? These issues question the validity of the theory.

The placement of sexuality also poses a problem for the theory. Sexuality is firmly assigned to the first tier as a physiological need like hunger, thirst, and breathing. W.B. Cannon's *The Wisdom of the Body*[9] most likely served as the evidence that sexuality was merely a biological drive. What this placement ignores is the importance of sexuality in bonding between parent and child, loving relationships, and significantly, the role of sexuality in creativity and aesthetics.

Recent critics of Maslow's pyramid, in which self-actualization is placed at the top as the highest need, are seen as ethnocentric. According to Geert Hofstede,[10] Maslow's hierarchy of needs fails to illustrate and expand upon the difference between the social and intellectual needs of those raised in individualistic societies and those raised in collectivist societies. Individualist societies value the contributions of individuals, whereas collectivist societies value the contribution of the group. While this criticism of self-actualization has merit in contemporary society, the theory was developed in an era when psychology was based on the individual while sociology, a separate discipline, studied groups. However, any judgment of Maslow's needs hierarchy pyramid must also consider the exclusion of religion from the theory.

Religion

Human beings, Maslow believed, need something beyond themselves that they are connected to in a naturalistic sense, but not in a religious sense. As an atheist, Maslow found it anathema to accept religious experience as valid. Religion (*ligare*, to bind, Latin) has no mention in needs hierarchy theory except in the crude sense of spirituality. Throughout human history, religious motives and beliefs have bound man to God and to his fellow man; yet Maslow, the constructionist, built his own knowledge of religion. This shy, depressed, lonely, self-reflective, neurotic boy had little use for Yahweh, who was omnipotent, omnipresent, and all loving. Instead, he threw himself at the feet of strong and collegial Jewish scholars for direction. As a matter of fact, Kurt Goldstein had come up with self-actualization, which Maslow introduced in his 1943 *Psychological Review* paper. If you believe in the power of spiritual transcendence but do not believe in the source of spirituality, you believe in yourself. To echo the words of St. Augustine, if you believe what you like in the Gospels and reject what you don't like, it is not the Gospel you believe but yourself. As with much in psychology as a discipline, the study of human motivation has become a celebration of self.

Summary

Maslow's needs hierarchy established an alternative understanding of motivation from behaviorism and psychoanalysis and charted a course toward humanistic psychology. The needs consist of physiological, safety, belongingness, esteem, and the unique need of self-actualization, which stands at the peak of personal development. While extensive reviews of Maslow's theory found little evidence for its validity, nonetheless, it enjoys wide acceptance in pedagogy and among the public.

REFERENCES

1. Maslow, A. H. (1943). A theory of human motivation, *Psychological Review*, 370–396.
2. Maslow, 1943.
3. Maslow, A. H. (1954). *Motivation and personality*. New York: Harper.
4. Piaget, J. (1972). *The psychology of intelligence*. Routledge Classics (Vol. 92).
5. Maslow, A.H. (1962). *Toward a psychology of being*. New York: Van Nostrand.
6. Kaur, A. (2013). Maslow's need hierarchy theory: Applications and criticisms, *Global Journal of Management and Business Studies,* ISSN 2248-9878, *8*(10), 1061–1064.
7. Kurs, S. (2021). Maslow's hierarchy of needs in education. Education Library. https// Maslow's-hierarchy-of-needs-in-education.
8. Wahba, M.A., and Bridwell, L.G. (1976). Maslow reconsidered: A review of research on the need hierarchy theory. *Organizational Behavior and Human Performance*, *15*, 212–240. https://doi.org/10.1016/0030-5073(76)90038-6 tp://dx.doi.org/10.1016/0030-5073(76)90038-6
9. Cannon, W.B. (1932). *The Wisdom of the body*. London: Keegan Paul & Company.
10. Hofstede, G. (2016). National cultures in four dimensions, A research-based theory of cultural differences among nations. https://doi.org/10.1080/00208825.1983.11656358

TWENTY-FOUR

WITNESS TO TRUTH: A REVIEW

*Contradiction is not a sign of falsity, nor the lack
of contradiction a sign of truth.*
—Blaise Pascal

Lucas Graves (2016). *Deciding What's True: The Rise
of Political Fact-checking in American Journalism.*
Columbia University Press: New York.

"Practical politics consists in ignoring the facts," declared Henry Adams in the second volume of *The Education of Henry Adams.*" Too often, politicians, office holders, and candidates for office ignore, twist, distort, and disregard facts in their political discourse. Politicians sometimes behave as if the facts underlying their assertions are not important to an informed public.

According to author Lucas Graves, assistant professor of sociology at the University of Wisconsin, the response to these shortcomings in public discourse and the failure of the news media to fully reveal the veracity of their postings is the emergence of a new class of political fact-checkers—journalists who specialize in assessing public claims and communicate their findings to other journalists, politicians, activists, and the general public. *Deciding What's True* contends that the new fact-checkers constitute a reform movement that reaches to the core of American journalism. "How has the Internet—not as a technological force, but as a complex of affordances rendered meaningful by new practices, norms, and organizations—transformed journalistic work and the world of news production?" The new actors and behaviors reveal deeper currents in the practice of journalism and its defining professional norm.

While a graduate student, Lucas volunteered to intern and interview journalists at the elite fact-checking organizations (FactCheck. org, Polifact, *Washington Post's* Fact Checker) to learn the techniques of how factual veracity is uncovered and the public informed. His fact-checker training involved learning the matrix for choosing which facts to check, researching and deciding what is true, and conducting extended case studies in which the fact-checker as journalist draws on reason, judgment, and, ultimately, values to interpret a contested assertion and make a coherent assessment of where the truth lies. *Deciding What's True* hinges on Graves' experiences with the respected fact-checking organizations at which he worked; it is essentially an account of their motivations, practices, and results within the ecology of journalism.

Following the tradition set by Herb Gans in the classic work on news media, *Deciding What's News,* Graves dates the origins of professional fact-checking to December 9, 2011, when a blogger issued a call to arms against the mainstream news media: "It's 2001, and we can Fact Check your ass." The phrase quickly entered the meme blogosphere and became a rallying cry for the antagonism between bloggers and professional journalists. The internet afforded bloggers a medium for criticism that would take journalists to task for errors in reporting. And, of course, journalists would frequently counter these vacuous, off-the-cuff, superficial attacks on their own well-researched news accounts. Such was the heated climate in the ecosphere of news reporting, which included bloggers, journalists, activists, commentators, and the news organizations. The veracity of news accounts was often called to question in blogs, with rebuttals and counterclaims by journalists. It was within this milieu, that FactCheck.org was established in 2003 and PolitiFact and *The Washington Post*'s Fact Checker both were founded in 2007 to bring professional fact-checking to journalism. Graves describes the newswork of fact-checkers thus:

> Fact-checkers scan the news and pore over transcripts looking for suspicious claims; they trace the media origins of political rumors and bogus political career of these claims; and they promote their conclusions eagerly to other journalists, encouraging news outlets to cite their findings and to invite them on the air. Fact-checkers do, in one sense, assume the journalist's traditional role as witness: They witness and report on mediated events. Fact-checkers are both students of and participants in a news ecosystem which assembles news, and constructs authority through citation and annotation of other media.

Document exegesis is the core of a professional fact-checker's newswork. Graves terms this activity annotative journalism, which he defines as journalism that proceeds mainly through the critical analysis of published texts, be they news accounts, official documents, or other publicly available texts.

> Like bloggers, they exploit the affordances of hypertext for citation and annotation, for linking and quoting and excerpting. Their style of newswork is profoundly intertextual and relies on formal and informal ties to other news organizations. Fact-checkers draw on published news accounts as a source both of dubious claims and of the evidence to check

those claims, while they encourage other news outlets to cite their research. Fact-checkers pay avid attention to the traces their work leaves through the news ether, and to how it is assessed by journalists, political figures, high-profile bloggers, and the wider online public.

Once a dubious claim is uncovered, it is made available to the news media to be shared with the public. Fact-checkers often question the effects of their newswork. Does fact-checking actually improve the veracity of public discourse? Do politicians actually pay attention to the facts in their debates, advertisements, public statements? With the inception of fact-checking, has truthfulness flourished in what appears in the press and media?

Graves believes that fact-checking has the potential to effect change in three different ways for three different audiences. First, a fact-check may provide information that corrects an erroneous belief or immunizes the reader against false claims and perhaps changes their thinking. Second, fact-checking may encourage other journalists to challenge falsehoods and adjudicate factual debates rather than just report competing "he said/she said" views. Finally, fact-checking may, as a consequence of its effects on public opinion or press coverage, inhibit political lying by making it more costly for public figures to distort the truth. At professional fact-checking conferences, examples of such positive results are proffered in small numbers. However, the public's notice of fact-checking reports seemingly grows logarithmically.

Fact-checkers claim that it is not their mission to moralize or clean up the lies in the cultural landscape—"Just the facts ma'am," as uttered by Jack Webb in almost every episode of the TV series "Dragnet." Fact-checkers are not the police of fraudulent or corrupt public discourse. Rather, their role is to make known false or misleading claims so that what Herb Gans has called "journalism's theory of democracy" aids citizens to make well-informed choices at the ballot box.

As an engaged participant and concerned academician, Graves has offered an in-depth history of professional fact-checking from its inception. The landscape, work, and effects of this new class of journalists who assess public claims are placed within the wider context of journalism to assure us, the public, that politicians do not ignore the facts.

TWENTY-FIVE

THE GREEK REVOLUTION: 1821 THE MAKING OF MODERN EUROPE[1]

Greece, a land with a special destiny, Freedom's Home, or Glory's grave.
—Lord Byron

T wo hundred years have passed since twenty-year-old Anagnostis Zymaras, my great-great- grandfather, joined the company of Kapetan Kostas Katsikas along with other peasants to overthrow the Ottoman tyranny in Peloponnesus. Little did Anagnostis envision that two centuries later the eminent historian of the Balkans, Mark Mazower, would chronicle the revolution that followed and conclude that the independence of Greece had far-reaching effects on nationalist movements throughout Europe.

On or around March 25, 1821, what began as against-the-odds uprisings in several places in Morea (Peloponnesus) and Rumelia to the North, resulted in a coming together of disjointed, poorly armed

Greek patriots under the quarreling headship of notable land and ship owners, who often placed the interests of their clan above the goal of a united Greek nation. Dysfunctional leadership cost the revolt its early gains and prolonged the war.

The uprising led to ethnic cleansing of both Muslims and Christians. While seen as a war between Greek versus Turk or Christian versus Muslim actually the conflict was more complicated. In Rumelia the relation between the Greek armatoles (Christian) and Albanian beys (Muslim) found them sometimes at odds with each other and sometimes in league against a common enemy. Enemies in appearance only and living together in Rumelia, they were sometimes forgetful of their duties to nation or religion. Nonetheless, a brutal war continued for twelve years.

By 1823, the two sides seemed locked in a never-ending struggle in which neither side could defeat the other. The Greeks dominated the Morea, but they had failed to drive the Ottomans out of the few remaining fortresses that they held, let alone to sue for peace. The Ottomans could mount campaigns on an annual basis but lacking a regular army or properly commanded navy, these could not reestablish the empire's authority. Both sides, therefore, began casting about for allies whose contributions might be decisive (p.213).

Greek tactics were largely hit and run, yet sustained the war effort. In spite of crushing a superior Ottoman force at Aráchova, near Delphi, the Greeks were unable to take Patras and Athens, supplied as they were by Ottoman materiel and reinforcements. Mazower's magisterial historical account brings to life the men and women who brought about the emergence of Greece and those Europeans and Americans who assisted in its victory.

When a weak power faces an unquestionably strong power, success of the weaker is unlikely without outside intervention. This was certainly the case of the American colonies against England. France's assistance and its fleet turned the tide for the Americans. Likewise, the intercession of Europeans served the Greek cause. The Greek revolution became a worldwide liberal cause célèbre, romantic in spirit, and reclaiming the glory of ancient Hellas.

Gold from London and loans from France financed the Greek war effort. A motley group of European adventurers assembled to join the Greek cause with mixed results. Tabloids in European capitals broadcast the enslavement of women and children. Books, letters, papers, periodicals, speeches in parliament persuaded influential Europeans of the justice of the Greek cause. Artist Eugène Delacroix depicted the misery of the Chios massacre, Henri Decisisae the fall of Mesolonghi, both of which outraged European elites and provoked the legendary Lord George Gordon Byron to join the ranks in Mesolonghi and die tragically on its shores.

A surrogate Egyptian army was sent to Peloponnesus under the command of Ibrahim Pasha, who in a sense held the fate of the Ottoman Empire in his hands. His mission was to wreak havoc on its economy, villages and populace of the Morea. Having destroyed Tripolitsa, Ibrahim happened to encounter some British travelers and he described his task to them:

He would burn and destroy the whole Morea so that it neither be profitable to the Greeks nor to him, nor to anyone, . . . His father Mehmet Ali was training forty thousand men and he was in daily expectation of twelve thousand. If these were cut off, he would have more; and he would persevere till the Greeks returned to their former state. One of the castles on the plain, he said, had been carried by the assault, and the garrison all put to the sword, the other was expected to fall immediately. He repeated: I will not cease till Morea be a ruin. (p.298)

Meanwhile the movement for intervention on behalf of the Greeks was gaining momentum among the major powers. The Treaty of London (1827), signed by Britain, France, Russia, and the Greeks but rejected by Constantinople, laid the foundations for an autonomous Greece. The destruction of the Ottoman and Egyptian fleets by a combined British, French, and Russian fleet in the Bay of Navarino for all intents and purposes put an end to the Ottoman cause in

Greece. Ibrahim was forced to remove his troops from the Morea. After several years of negotiations with the Sultan, a treaty was signed, and in 1833 the Bavarian Prince Otto von Wittelsbach was enthroned King of Greece.

What sets apart Mazower's magnificent and thoroughly researched history of the Greek Revolution from the many other fine accounts of the war is that it places the conflict in the wider context of the evolving nation state. The successful Greek revolt was a harbinger of a profound transformation of European Society. The uprising of 1821 came after nearly a half century of revolts starting with the American colonies, the overthrow of the French monarchy, and Haiti's bid for freedom. Following Napoleon's defeat and exile, the table was set for a breakup of empires and the formation of nation states. Europe was in turmoil, with uprisings in Spain, Sicily, Naples, and Piedmont, which were readily put down. Only the Greek revolt, after a dozen pitiless years of travail and violence, managed to separate the region from the Ottoman Empire and establish a nation state unified in language, religion, and democratic rule.

What followed was a unification in the course of the nineteenth century of other subject peoples—Italians, Poles, and Germans—who saw the success of the Greeks as a promise for their future. Empires and principalities began coming apart, with the Ottoman in the lead. By the mid-twentieth century, nation-states rather than empires and monarchies made up the world.

The Treaty of London brought major powers together to mediate a conflict far from their shores, but close to their interests. Today the United States on its own is unable to effect peace in the Ukraine, but the great powers of that day, in unity, were able to bring the conflict between the Ottoman Empire and the rebellious Greeks to closure. But violence was required to end the violence in Morea and Rumelia. A new international system evolved from the deliberations on the Greek War and how to bring about peace. Mazower suggests that a century ago, the founding of the League of Nations, precursor of the United Nations, served as the basis of today's conflict resolution among nation states.

No records list Anagnostis Zymaras in military service in 1828. He had married, and the first of three children, Athanasios, was born that year. A man of substance, Anagnostis was best man at the wedding of Giorgios Kostakis of Tsitalia and Theodora Hontzas on July 1, 1845 in Kosmas, Arcadia. Greece was a nation at peace.

It is fitting that this story of my Greek identity begins with the story of Anagnostis Zymaras and ends with this chronicle of the Greek Revolutionary War in which my great-great-grandfather fought and survived. Greek identity came into existence with the end of the war and was carried in the diaspora to the United States.

REFERENCE

1. Mazower, M. (2021). *The Greek revolution 1821 and the making of modern Europe*. Penguin Random House.

EPILOGUE

My End Is My Beginning and My Beginning Is My End

At age 85, we are much like a debenture to be called in, according to Fay Vincent, the former commissioner of baseball, who shares my age. Indeed, I accumulated many debts in my reckless youth, and this chronicle barely covers the depths of my indebtedness or the heights of my gratitude. My love and later loss of my brother David seared my heart. His *philotimia*, in the care of our parents, his support of our sister, Peggy, and his counsel to me while conflicted as I pursued an academic career was profound. He was a noble, self-sacrificing son and brother.

My parents were visiting Doulie and me in New York when we received tragic word from my sister that David was killed in a car accident in northern Indiana on July 4, 1978. The accident was not far from our Aunt Angelike's diner, near the road that carried me and dad home as I bawled my heart out. My mournful tears had been shed in the coffee truck 35 years before. We all rushed back to Chicago, made the arrangements for the funeral, and grieved. Father Nicholas Nikokavouras came to our parents' home and performed a service to heal our broken hearts. We were all in arrested attention as he performed the rite and prayers. Later, Doulie said that she felt David's presence in the room as we prayed for his soul. Doulie and I were childless during our first seven years of marriage; ten months after David's death our first child, Sofia, was born. Death precedes life.

A bright painting, by Edward Sokol, depicting the interior of the artist's studio, graces our family room. The elements of the painter's tools are scattered here and there: brushes, a pallet, canvases, tubes of paint, and rags smeared with paint dabs. The artist also tended vibrant plants and flowers, and his artworks were in a jumble throughout the studio. In the center of the painting is the artist's easel bearing an untouched, blank canvas, which commands the attention of the viewer. The painting was purchased about a year before I finished this book. I stared at the white canvas and pondered the writing labor ahead. Empiricist philosophers characterize the beginning of life as a *tabula rasa*, a clean slate. Indeed, the blank canvas beckoned me to begin this story of my youthful life after a man with his dog stopped by a park bench where I was reading and asked, "Are you Greek?" So, I opened a blank page on my computer and picked out some early memories, tattered family photos, Greek aphorisms, an evocative yearbook and a jumble of published essays and I began writing. This memoir ends with the storied Greek Revolution, which was the beginning of the Zimmar family tree when Anagnostis Zymaras picked up his rifle in 1821 AD to gain freedom from tyranny.

As my debenture becomes due, my end lies firmly in my beginnings.

ACKNOWLEDGMENTS

A scribbler needs an unscrambler to comb out the tangled assaults to syntax, semantics, and sense. When the editor is also a muse to guide the scrawler to a coherent narrative, what more can an author ask? Joanne Freeman has gone through every word in this manuscript, and my other essays and has consistently produced truly impactful content. Moreover, Joanne superb editorial skills came with our friendship, which is more precious to me than anything that I have written. Mnemosyne in Greek mythology was the goddess of memory. That role fell on my sister, Peggy Zimmar, when I was befogged as to the time and events of our years growing up in Chicago. David Hicks, a philhellene, and a true Orthodox brother in Christ, encouraged me to bring Greek traditions to the text and into my life. As I searched for memoirs by Greek Americans, self-publisher of *Don't Marry an American*, Ben Kyriagis, offered counsel. His first comment on my manuscript was that it won't sell because the narrative widely missed the audience for such books. He was especially helpful in bringing market clarity to the text and bringing it closer to its readers. Michel Hersen and I hail back to graduate school as co-researchers, but then, he set me to writing short stories as we entered retirement from teaching. Dr. Fernando Espi Forcén, founder and editor of the *Journal of Humanistic Psychiatry*, provided the incentive to develop essays on the interstice between psychology and humanism. Gregory Kondos, of *Greek Ancestry* supplied the impetus for this memoir when he uncovered the deeds of my great, great grandfather Anagnostis Athanasios Zymaras (aka Zoumaras) as he prepared to do battle in the Greek Revolution in Peloponnesus in 1821, AD. The story of our family followed. My pilot in marriage, Doulie, is the guide, who makes loving each other so much a part of a meaningful life together.

www.ingramcontent.com/pod-product-compliance
Lightning Source LLC
Chambersburg PA
CBHW071150130626
46553CB00004B/1600